The

HERITAGE BOOK
2004

The HERITAGE BOOK *2004*

Edna McCann

HarperCollins*Publishers*Ltd

The author gratefully acknowledges the
following sources: "April" from RIVERS
TO THE SEA by SARA TEASDALE. The
poems "So Many Walk . . . ," "To Those
Who Are Content" and "Autumn Flight"
are from LIGHT OF THE YEARS by
GRACE NOLL CROWELL. © 1936 by
Harper & Row, Publishers, Inc. ©
renewed 1964 by GRACE NOLL
CROWELL. Reprinted by permission of
HarperCollins Publishers Inc. "Stepping
Ashore" from BETTER THAN GOLD by
ROBERT E. SELLE. "This I Know"
from AIM FOR A STAR by HELEN
LOWRIE MARSHALL. "Let There Be
Peace On Earth" by JILL JACKSON and
SY MILLER. © 1955, 1983 by Jan-Lee
Music. Reproduced courtesy of Jan-Lee
Music.

HarperCollins Publishers Ltd. has made
every effort to find the holders of copy-
righted materials published in this book.
Any questions regarding permissions
should be addressed to the publisher.

First Edition

HarperCollins books may be purchased
for educational, business, or sales promo-
tional use through our Special Markets
Department.

HarperCollins Publishers Ltd.
2 Bloor Street East, 20th Floor
Toronto, Ontario, Canada
M4W 1A8

www.harpercanada.com

National Library of Canada Cataloguing
in Publication

McCann, Edna
The Heritage Book / Edna McCann
Annual.
1st ed. (1977)–
Issues for 2000– published by
HarperCollins.
ISSN 0711-4737
ISBN 0-00-200662-6 (2004 edition)

1. Anecdotes. 2. Maxims, English.
I. Title.

PN6331.M32   242'.2   C82-030470-0

TC 9 8 7 6 5 4 3 2 1

Printed and bound in Canada
Set in New Caledonia

Introduction

And so another year begins. As a young woman, I often took this event for granted. Now, in my "golden years," I have a much greater appreciation for this momentous occasion.

How wonderful it is to have the chance to see the new year begin, with its opportunities to share new experiences, to learn, to grow and to live every day with joy.

So much has happened in the last few years; the world has changed with dizzying speed, and yet I find in conversations with family and friends, and with letters from my readers, that people have changed very little. Values like courage, kindness, tolerance, hard work and honesty are still highly esteemed. Young people have dreams, and it seems everyone continues to maintain faith and hope in the future, just as we did when I was young.

I hope that this year's *Heritage Book 2004* will provide you with many happy moments, and that you, too, will see this year as the miracle that it is.

Edna McCann

The

HERITAGE BOOK
2004

January

Thursday January 1

To the New Year

To leave the old with a burst of song;
To recall the right and forgive the wrong;
To forget the things that bind you fast
To the vain regrets of the year that's past;

To have the strength to let go your hold
Of the not worth while of the days of old;
To dare to go forth with a purpose true
To the unknown task of the year that's new.

To help your brother along the road
To do his work and lift his load;
To add your gift to the world's good cheer
Is to have and give a Happy New Year.

Author unknown

On New Year's Day many of us recall the joys and sorrows, and the successes and failures, of the past 12 months. We look forward to the coming year with hope and are often inspired to make New Year's resolutions that, by some miracle, we may be able to keep.

SKATERS' WALTZ

I enjoy this thought from Scott McConnell:

Every resolution that you make on this day implies that you are in control of yourself, that you are not a victim fated by circumstances, controlled by stars, owned by luck, but that you are an individual who can make choices to change your life.

May your resolutions inspire you and may you enjoy a year of good health and happiness.

Friday January 2

The world is full of wonders, riches, powers, puzzles. What it holds can make us horrified, amazed, sorrowful, confused, joyful. But nothing in it can make us bored. Boredom is the result of some pinch in ourselves, not of some lack in the world.

Toni Flores

Saturday January 3

My daughter Julia is an executive in a large corporation and frequently travels around the world to company meetings. Although she enjoys travelling, there are many times when circumstances cause inconveniences that she would rather avoid.

Someone in Julia's office handed out this amusing list of "Things you wish you would hear when travelling . . . but probably never will."

1. We'll be arriving much ahead of schedule today.
2. To the flight attendant, "That meal was simply delicious!"
3. We seem to have damaged your luggage. Let us replace it for you.
4. Your room isn't available yet. Would you consider upgrading to a suite at our expense?
5. Golly, here's room service already.
6. We don't feel our service was up to standard, so your entire stay is complimentary.

Sunday January 4

For I am persuaded that neither death, nor life, nor angels, nor principalities, nor powers, nor things present, nor things to come, nor height, nor depth, nor any other creature, shall be able to separate us from the love of God, which is Christ Jesus our Lord.

Romans 8:38–39

Monday January 5

It's nice, after the hectic pace of the holiday season, to spend some quiet time alone. As I grow older (and more deaf), I find the noise and confusion of our family gatherings to be somewhat overwhelming.

So it was with great pleasure today that I set a fire in the fireplace and sat down in my favourite chair to read one of the many new books that I received as Christmas gifts.

Although I read books of all types with pleasure, many of my favourites are either mysteries or stories written by humorists.

I found myself laughing out loud many times this afternoon and, by this evening, realized that I was feeling very refreshed.

Laughter really is good medicine!

Tuesday January 6

Today is Epiphany, a day celebrating the visit of the Three Wise Men to the infant Jesus.

Where is he that is born King of the Jews? For we have seen his star in the east and have come to worship him.

Matthew 2:2

Wednesday January 7

Many of us know the minor frustration of pausing during a conversation to try to recall the perfect word to finish our thought—the word that is right on the tip of our tongue, but annoyingly out of reach. Now try to imagine the hopelessness of not being able to recall your own name, the face of a loved one, or even how to perform such everyday tasks as dressing oneself.

Tragically, this is reality for people suffering from Alzheimer's disease. A degenerative ailment that attacks the brain, Alzheimer's disease impairs thinking, memory and behaviour. As the disease progresses, sufferers may become disoriented, have difficulty with performing familiar tasks and often show decreased or poor judgment.

Most distressing may be personality changes. Nearly all of us know someone whose life has been affected by Alzheimer's disease, but until one has cared for a loved one with this disease, it's difficult to comprehend how devastating it can be.

The physical and emotional demands of caring for a loved one with Alzheimer's, especially as the disease progresses, can be overwhelming.

Thankfully here in Canada, we can turn to the Alzheimer's Society for help. Founded in 1978, the Alzheimer's Society has expanded to serve Canadians from coast to coast. The three major goals—family support, education and research—were recognized early, and today the society offers help for those dealing with Alzheimer's disease.

The Alzheimer's Society needs volunteers in many capacities. If you or someone you know has time to be involved there is an ever increasing need for people to assist and support the families dealing with this devastating disease.

Thursday January 8

Not all of us have to possess earth-shaking talent. Just common sense and love will do.

Myrtle Auvil

Friday January 9

For the people of the Iroquois nation, the New Year begins five days after the first new moon in January. The Midwinter Festival lasts for eight days and is celebrated by wearing traditional clothing, feasting, dancing and participating in games and chanting ceremonies. The ceremonies are often held in the longhouse or the community centre. In years past, the Iroquois hunters stocked the longhouse with a large supply of meat for the festival. Boiled beef and venison are still a popular part of this feast.

There is a restored Iroquois village at the Crawford Lake Conservation Area in rural Milton, Ontario, not far from Toronto. Originally discovered in 1792, the settlement has been heralded as one of the most interesting discoveries in Native history. A large portion of the village has been reproduced to exact specifications from its origins (estimated to be between 1434 and 1459).

During the Midwinter Festival, the Iroquois beg the Creator for life and for the continuity of their lives in tune with the rhythms of nature.

❖   ❖   ❖

What is life? It is the flash of a firefly in the night. It is the breath of a buffalo in the wintertime. It is the little shadow which runs across the grass and loses itself in the sunset.

Crowfoot, Blackfoot chief
(on his deathbed in 1890)

Saturday January 10

What makes a happy life? With each individual this answer will vary, but I believe that these words from George Bernard Shaw apply to everyone:

This is the true joy in life, the being used for a purpose recognized by yourself as a mighty one; the being thoroughly worn out before you are thrown on the scrap heap; the being a force of nature instead of a feverish little clod of ailments and grievances, complaining that the world will not devote itself to making you happy.

Sunday January 11

Ah, dearest Jesus, holy Child,
Make thee a bed, soft, undefiled,
Within my heart, that it may be
A quiet chamber, kept for thee.

Martin Luther

Monday January 12

> We must live through the weary winter,
> If we would value spring.
> And the woods must be cold and silent,
> Before the robins sing.
>
> The flowers must be buried in darkness,
> Before they can bud and bloom.
> And the sweetest and warmest sunshine
> Comes after the storm and gloom.
>
> So the heart, from the hardest trial,
> Gains the purest joy of all.
> And from the lips that have tasted sadness
> The sweetest songs will fall.
>
> For as peace comes after suffering,
> And love is reward of pain,
> So, after earth, comes heaven,
> And out of our loss, the gain.

My thanks to the unknown author.

Tuesday January 13

Since reading is the basis on which most of our education is built, it is crucial that children develop a love of books and reading. Wise parents recognize the importance of reading and will begin a nightly ritual of a bedtime story—even with tiny infants.

I believe that a love of reading is the greatest gift my parents gave me. I have tried to pass this same love on to my children, grandchildren and great-grandchildren.

Wednesday January 14

During the extremely cold weather at this time of year, there are many different suggestions about how to keep warm without racking up staggering utility bills.

Thermal underwear, unlike the old thick and itchy "long johns," is thin, easily worn under clothing and extremely warm. In bed, the good old flannel sheet is a warm comfort, as is a hot water bottle for the feet (for those who don't care for an electric blanket).

Eating well also helps keep you warm. Something hot for breakfast as well as warm drinks throughout the day keep the chill away.

I often keep a fire going in my fireplace and when all else fails, I sit beside it and read letters from my friend Emily, who winters in Florida. There's something about putting your thoughts on a beach that seems to warm the whole body.

Thursday January 15

Today is the birth date of Martin Luther King, Jr., the late American inspirational civil rights leader. Instrumental in introducing the strategy of civil disobedience to the black struggle for equality, Dr. King remains an icon for African-Americans to this day.

Power at its best is love implementing the demands of justice. Justice at its best is love correcting everything that stands against love.

Martin Luther King, Jr., 1963

Friday January 16

Take a chance! All life is a chance. The man who goes farthest is generally the one who is willing to do and dare. The "sure thing" boat never gets far from shore.

Dale Carnegie

Saturday January 17

On a cold and miserable winter's night is there anything nicer than a bowl of hot soup—and a hockey game to watch on television? In our home, Saturday night was *Hockey Night in Canada*. My husband, George, would make his famous chili, and the girls and I would gather around the radio and listen to Foster Hewitt call out, "He shoots, he scores!" as we cheered on our Toronto Maple Leafs. This evening I'll be cheering for "my boys" as I enjoy Swiss Cheese Soup.

Swiss Cheese Soup

1 onion
4 bacon slices
2 pints (1 L) chicken stock (or broth)
8 oz. (250 g) Emmenthaler cheese, grated
4 cups (1 L) fresh white bread crumbs
1 1/4 cups (300 mL) dry white wine
3 tbsp. (45 mL) each chopped chives, parsley, chervil and salt (to taste)

1. Peel the onion and slice very thinly.
2. In a fry pan, cook bacon until crisp, remove and keep warm. Add the sliced onions to the bacon fat and cook until golden brown. Remove and keep warm with the bacon.
3. Heat the chicken stock to boiling. Put the grated cheese with the bread crumbs in a

warmed soup tureen. Pour the boiling stock into the tureen and leave to soak for 3 minutes, stirring occasionally. The bread crumbs should disintegrate and the cheese melt.

4. Stir in wine, herbs and salt (to taste). Garnish with the bacon and onion and serve immediately.

Makes 4 servings.

Sunday January 18

Lord, keep my parents in your love
Lord, bless them and keep them.
Lord, please let me have money
And strength and keep my parents
for many years
So that I can take care of them.
Amen

The prayer of a young
Ghanian Christian

Monday January 19

As I am well aware, one can never know everything there is to be known about human nature. One can be sure only of one thing, and that is that it will never cease to have a surprise in store for you.

W. Somerset Maugham

Tuesday January 20

My friend Jake Frampton stopped by for dinner this evening. Our friendship goes back so many years that it is more like having a family member over for dinner than "company."

In her book *Skimming the Cream*, Zula Bennington Greene wrote: "Some feel honoured when they are put at a table where the best linen and china are laid out. But the ones who are really honoured are the ones who are set at a table where the dishes and the eating utensils are recruited from the kitchen. They are the true and trusted friends who do not need to be complimented or impressed and who would never think of criticizing."

Jake is an "unmatched dishes" friend with whom I am completely comfortable—a rare treasure indeed.

Wednesday January 21

I pack my trunk, embrace my friends, embark on the sea, and at last wake up in Naples, and there beside me is the Stern Fact, the Sad Self, unrelenting, identical, that I fled from.

Ralph Waldo Emerson

Thursday January 22

My sister, Sarah, and her husband, Richard, live on Canada's East coast. I grew up in the area and there are still times when I miss not only the sounds and sights of the seacoast, but also the people, whose kindness and sense of community are very well known.

Sarah likes to tell this story to illustrate the East coast generosity that has become legendary.

Several years ago, two young university students were heading home to Montreal when they ran out of gas. They hitchhiked to the closest service station, where they explained their plight to the attendant and asked for a can of gas. As the young men paid for the gas, the attendant told them that there was a ten-dollar security fee for the can. Somewhat upset at this lack of trust, they headed for the door, and the long walk back to their car in the driving snow and sub-zero temperatures.

"Wait a minute," the attendant called as he looked out at the storm, "you shouldn't walk far in weather like this." He pulled a set of keys from his pocket. "Take my car," he insisted.

Friday January 23

> Age is like a mountain high,
> Rare is the air, and blue;
> A long hard climb and
> A little fatigue
> But oh! What a beautiful view.
>
> *Author unknown*

Saturday January 24

From the time he was a child, my grandson Marshall has been interested in unusual trivia or little-known facts. With the advent of computers, Marshall's curiosity knows no bounds, and he frequently enjoys letting the rest of us in on some new-found information. Perhaps you'll impress your friends with this tidbit of knowledge.

Should you find yourself looking for food in the African bush, you need to follow the calls of the honey-guide, a drab little bird that will lead the way to honey hives it has found.

Strangely, this bird needs humans, as it is unable to break into the hives that it finds. It will seek out people and fly ahead, a bit at a time, waiting for them to catch up. Having arrived at the hive, the bird will wait on a nearby branch for the hive to be opened. African folklore requires that one leave a piece of the honeycomb for the honey-guide. It is thought that if you fail to do so, the next time the honey-guide might lead you to a lion's den (or something worse).

Sunday January 25

What a friend we have in Jesus,
all our sins and griefs to bear!
What a privilege to carry
everything to God in prayer!

Oh, what peace we often forfeit,
oh, what needless pain we bear,
All because we do not carry
everything to the Lord in prayer!

Monday January 26

Yesterday, Scots everywhere gathered to honour the memory of Robbie Burns. So much has been said, written and sung that anything I might write is repetitious.

Something that has always been a part of this Scottish festivity is haggis. For most Canadians, haggis is a mystery, not unlike the Loch Ness monster—something that is only in Scotland. You may learn more than you want to know about haggis by reading a description of it in the Oxford dictionary.

Believe me when I tell you that it tastes every bit as awful as it sounds!

My daughter Marg insists that it perfectly fitting to honour Robbie Burns on his special day by humming "Auld Lang Syne" in your head. Those of Scottish origin may not agree!

Tuesday January 27

Listening is as important as talking. If you are a good listener, people often compliment you for being a good conversationalist.

Governor Jesse Ventura

Wednesday January 28

I enjoy Dave Barry's sense of humour:

I argue very well. Ask any of my remaining friends. I can win an argument on any topic. People know this and steer clear of me at parties. Often, as a sign of their great respect, they don't even invite me.

Thursday January 29

A lot of people are like wheelbarrows—no good unless pushed. Some are like trailers—they have to be pulled. Some are like kites—if you don't keep a string on them, they will fly away. Some are like balloons—full of wind and ready to blow up. Some are like footballs—you can't tell which way they will bounce. And then some are like a good watch—open-faced, pure gold, quietly busy and full of good works.

Friday January 30

Why doesn't the fellow who says, "I'm no speechmaker" let it go at that instead of giving a demonstration?

K. Hubbard

Saturday January 31

Courage is what it takes to stand up and speak; courage is also what it takes to sit down and listen.

February

Sunday February 1

When morning gilds the skies,
My heart awaking cries,
May Jesus Christ be praised!
Alike at work and prayer
To Jesus I repair;
May Jesus Christ be praised!

Whene'er the sweet church bell
Peals over the hill and dell,
May Jesus Christ be praised!
O hark to what it sings,
As joyously it rings,
May Jesus Christ be praised!

Rev. E. Caswall
(translated from the German)

Monday February 2

This is a day that I enjoy very much. It is the one day a year when we "conservative" Canadians feel free to be just a little silly. After all, how often do people rely on a groundhog to predict the coming weather?

In fact, the origination of Groundhog Day came from the ancient belief that hibernating creatures were able to predict the arrival of spring. This, coupled with Candlemas Day, which falls halfway between winter solstice and spring equinox, has become the prognosticator for the weather for the next six weeks.

If Candlemas Day be fair and bright,
Winter will have another flight,
But if it be dark with clouds and rain,
Winter is gone and will not come again.

Tuesday February 3

Just a year ago, on the first day of this month, the world suffered a devastating loss when the space shuttle *Columbia* blew up while re-entering the earth's atmosphere. The seven crew members, astronauts whose courage and daring set them apart, were all lost in the tragic accident.

The *Columbia* was on a 16-day mission devoted to research. The work included more than 80 experiments that studied earth and space science, advanced technology development and, ironically, astronaut safety.

For the most part, we had become rather blasé about space travel, and it was unlikely that many people even knew the names of the crew members before *Columbia*'s liftoff. Sadly, their names would become all too familiar as the investigation into the tragedy began.

President Bush spoke shortly after the accident:

"*Columbia* is lost; there are no survivors. In an age when space flight has come to seem almost routine, it is easy to overlook the dangers of travel by rocket, and the difficulties of navigating the fierce atmosphere of the Earth. These astronauts knew the dangers, and they faced them willingly, knowing they had a high and noble purpose.

"The same Creator who names the stars also knows the names of the seven souls we mourn today. The crew of the shuttle *Columbia* did not return safely to earth; yet we can pray that all are safely home."

Rick Husband, William McCool, Ilan Ramon, Kalpana Chawla, David Brown, Michael Anderson, Laurel Clark, heroes all; remember them well.

Wednesday February 4

If you sit down at the set of sun
And count the acts that you have done
And, counting, find
One self-denying deed, one word
That eased the heart of him who heard
One glance most kind,
That fell like sunshine where it went—
Then you may count that day well spent.

George Eliot

Thursday February 5

The nasty weather today reminded me of a funny story that my neighbour John told me several years ago.

A buddy of John's, a police officer, was on patrol when he noticed a car driving erratically down the road. The officer turned on his siren and pulled the car over, but not before the car had several near misses with other cars.

Noticing the ice-covered windshield, the policeman asked, "Wouldn't it help if you cleaned off your windshield?"

"I don't really think so," replied the little old lady who was driving. "You see, I left my glasses at home."

Friday February 6

The true test of friendship is to be able to sit or walk with a friend for an hour in perfect silence without wearying of one another's company.

D.M. Mulock Craik

Saturday February 7

My son-in-law Bruce has been ill the last few days with "strep throat"—a streptococcus infection causing a severe sore throat. The doctor has given him an antibiotic, tetracycline, and he is feeling much better today. If you have ever taken this particular medication, you may find today's story of interest.

Dr. Ben Duggar, a botany professor, was 70 years old in 1943 when the University of Wisconsin informed him that he had to retire. Though Dr. Duggar protested that he was a "young" 70, the university had a rule that retirement was mandatory at age 70. Although Duggar stepped down, he was bitterly disappointed.

Several of Duggar's graduates were working at Lederle Laboratories. They spoke to the head of the company and Dr. Duggar was hired as a consultant and independent researcher for Lederle.

In the Lederle labs were thousands of small drawers with samples of earth from all over the world. They needed to be cross-matched and nurtured into growing moulds. This meant nearly 36 million cross-matchings. Duggar was assigned to the task. After an uneventful first year, he isolated the antibiotic aureomycin. From this he developed tetracycline—the wonder antibiotic. At 73 years of age, he may well have saved more lives than any physician in history, all because he was forced to retire.

Sunday February 8

O give thanks to the Lord, for he is gracious: for his mercy endureth forever.

Psalm 118:29

Monday February 9

My good friend Marcia lives in Boston and, as you probably know, Boston has many lovely old churches.

Some years ago, Marcia was attending a Sunday service and before the service began, she was thumbing idly through the old hymn book in her pew. She found a tattered piece of paper on which she found the following written:

On this day—mend a quarrel. Search out a forgotten friend. Dismiss a suspicion and replace it with trust. Keep a promise. Forget an old grudge. Fight for a principle. Express your gratitude. Overcome an old fear. Take a few minutes to appreciate the beauty of nature. Tell someone you love him.

What wonderful advice!

Tuesday February 10

A wise parent lets a child know what is expected of him.

Author unknown

In the tiny village of St. Aniset, Quebec, Mr. and Mrs. Ernest Leger, shopkeepers, showed great faith in their two sons. Instead of doling out their allowance, the parents left the store's cash box open, allowing the boys to help themselves to their designated sums.

Some villagers felt this was an unfair temptation and told the parents so. The Legers saw it as a daily testament to their faith and trust.

It would seem that their faith was justified. The older son, Paul Emile, became a cardinal in the Catholic Church. The younger son, Jules, became a governor general of Canada.

Wednesday February 11

In his inimitable fashion, Mark Twain wrote his ideas on good health:

The only way to keep your health is to eat what you don't want, drink what you don't like, and do what you'd rather not.

Everyone seems to have an opinion of what promotes good health. My husband, George, and I made an effort to eat in moderation and to exercise regularly.

Horace, in 65 B.C., wrote, "Now learn what and how great benefits a temperate diet will bring along with it. In the first place you will enjoy good health."

"The groundwork of all happiness is health," according to Leigh Hunt.

Izaak Walton said, "Look to your health; and if you have it, praise God, and value it next to a good conscience: for health is the second blessing that we mortals are capable of; a blessing that money cannot buy."

Good health and good sense are two of life's greatest blessings.

From Publius Syrus (42 B.C.)

A man too busy to take care of his health is like a mechanic too busy to take care of his tools.

A Spanish Proverb

Thursday February 12

I went to visit my dear friend Lila McGuiness today. For the past several years Lila has lived in a nursing home, but because the home is so close, I'm able to get in to see her several times a week. Lila is a delightful lady—one of those marvellous people who takes life as it comes, never complaining; a joy to be with.

Today Lila and I were enjoying a cup of tea in the library when a young man came in with a beautiful yellow Labrador dog on a leash.

I was somewhat surprised, but Lila greeted both of them with enthusiasm. "Why, Kevin and Herschel . . . what brings you here today?"

As they spoke, Herschel had approached Lila's chair and was resting her head on Lila's lap, gazing at her with soulful brown eyes. Lila fondled the dog's ears as John explained, "The nurse called me to say that Mrs. Morelli was having a difficult day and she thought that Herschel may make her feel better."

People in the medical profession are turning

more and more to animals when patients have special needs. Even the most unwell patient will respond to a loving dog or cat. The animals seem to know who needs them the most and will gravitate to these patients, almost without exception.

After a few more scratches to the ears, Herschel and Kevin were off to visit Mrs. Morelli where, we hoped, he would provide some measure of comfort for a very sad lady.

Friday February 13

The trouble with giving advice is that some people want to repay you.

Saturday February 14

Valentine's Day

St. Valentine's Day, honouring St. Valentine, a Christian martyr who died in the third century, is a day that is special in many countries around the world. Here in Canada, the day is celebrated in a number of different ways. Cards, flowers, candy or gifts are just a few of the options for telling someone that you care.

One of the nicest Valentine's Days for our family came at a time when George and I had just moved to a new parish. We had three young daughters and little money, and were wondering what to do to celebrate.

A member of our new church arrived at our

home with a turkey dinner, complete with mashed potatoes, gravy, vegetables and dessert. Candles set in silver candleholders and a card reading "A Valentine welcome to you all" gave us a special Valentine that I have never forgotten.

Not all Valentines are this elaborate, but all are sent with love.

Sunday February 15

I will give thanks unto thee, O Lord, with my whole heart; I will speak of all thy marvellous works.

I will be glad and rejoice in thee: yea, my songs will I make of thy name, O thou most High.

Psalm 9:1–2

Monday February 16

It is a very curious fact that in bad days we can recall the good time that is now no more; but that in good days we have only a very cold and imperfect memory of the bad.

Arthur Schopenhauer

Tuesday February 17

Man strives for glory, honour, fame,
That all the world may know his name.
Amasses wealth by brain and hand;
Becomes a power in the land.
But when he nears the end of life
And looks back o'er the years of strife,
He finds that happiness depends
On none of these, but love of friends.

Author unknown

Wednesday February 18

This evening, Marg served a delicious beef stew for our dinner. When I was young, there wasn't a lot of money in our home, but my mother was incredibly good at making a little go a long way. Often the way that she did it was to make meals from the least expensive ingredients. She could take a tough old hen and make a chicken stew that melted in your mouth. Just thinking about her chicken stew with biscuits and gravy makes my mouth water.

The secret ingredient in Marg's stew is a touch of

curry powder. Those of you who have fond memories of any type of stew will certainly enjoy this recipe.

Marg's Special Beef Stew

4 lb. (2 kg) cubed stewing beef
1/2 (125 mL) cup flour
6 tbsp. (90 mL) cooking oil
1 large onion, sliced
2 tsp. (10 mL) salt
1/4 tsp. (1 mL) pepper
1 tsp. (5 mL) curry powder
1 clove garlic, minced
2 cups (500 mL) water
3 tbsp. (45 mL) chili sauce
1 bay leaf
hot cooked noodles

1. Roll the pieces of meat in the flour to coat all sides.
2. Heat the oil in a large heavy pan or Dutch oven. Add meat and brown well on all sides. Partway through the browning, add the onion, salt, pepper and curry powder. Continue browning, stirring constantly.
3. Add garlic, water, chili sauce and bay leaf. Bring mixture to a boil; turn down the heat, cover tightly and simmer until meat is tender (at least 2 hours). Remove the bay leaf. Serve over hot noodles.

Makes 8 servings.

Thursday February 19

I used the following selection a number of years ago, but one of my readers who just celebrated her 85th birthday asked if I would repeat it. Laura, this is for you.

Little drops of water,
Little grains of sand,
Make the mighty ocean
And the pleasant land.

So the little minutes
Humble though they be,
Make the mighty ages
Of eternity.

This poem from Julia Fletcher Carney is a reminder to all of us that time is precious. As I advance in years, this fact becomes more and more apparent to me.

As children we often wished time away. "When I'm six I can have a real bicycle." "I wish I were finished school." And so on. Do you remember?

As children we feel immortal. As seniors we feel our mortality all too well, as time flies by.

Constructive use of the time allotted to us may be our only way of slowing time's fleet passing.

It is said that the average person fritters away enough minutes to earn a college degree. Let's earn that college degree.

Friday February 20

Bernard Baruch made an interesting observation:

I will never be an old man. To me old age is always fifteen years older than I am.

Saturday February 21

Man cannot discover new oceans unless he has the courage to lose sight of the shore.

Sunday February 22

And as He was going along by the sea of Galilee, He saw Simon and Andrew, the brother of Simon, casting a net in the sea; for they were fishermen.

And Jesus said to them, "Follow me and I will make you fishers of men."

And they immediately left the nets and followed Him.

Mark 1:16–18

Monday February 23

February is designated as "Black History Month" in Canada. Originally it was called Negro History Week when it began in the United States in 1926. The month of February was chosen because it was the birth month of both U.S. president Abraham Lincoln and Frederick Douglass, a Maryland-born mulatto and runaway slave, whose book *Narrative of the Life of*

Frederick Douglass stirred sympathy in the North for escaped slaves.

Canada played a unique role in America's history. Our country was the end of the "underground railway," a prearranged route along which runaway slaves could come north to Canada and find freedom. It's estimated that 30,000 black slaves escaped as a result of this underground railway.

> I'm on my way to Canada,
> That cold and distant land,
> The dire effects of slavery,
> I can no longer stand.
> Farewell old master,
> Don't come after me.
> I'm on my way to Canada,
> Where coloured men are free.
>
> *"The Free Slave"*
> *A song by American Abolitionist*
> *George W. Clark*

Many of the men, women and children who arrived in Canada made their home in Elgin Settlement, in North Buxton, near Chatham, Ontario.

The Elgin Settlement is one of the few remaining black Canadian settlements that have been in existence since the pre-Civil War days. Today the settlement is inhabited, for the most part, by descendants of the original settlers who chose to remain in Canada.

Tuesday February 24

We say that we want to find God—well—suppose we did! We say we long to be assured that the Lord is with us—Well suppose suddenly you reached out your hand and felt Him! Suppose suddenly you lifted your eyes and saw Him looking down at you.

What would you do?

Peter Marshall

Wednesday February 25

Ash Wednesday

And now my friends, all that is true, all that is noble, all that is just and pure, all that is loveable and gracious; whatever is excellent and admirable—fill all your thoughts with these things.

Philippians 4:8

My husband, George, liked this biblical verse from Paul's letter to the Philippians as a guide for a positive Lenten season. He suggested using one of the six positive thoughts for each week of Lent. I try to follow his suggestion.

Thursday February 26

I had a very amusing thing happen this evening. I hope you'll find it so as well.

My daughter Julia has been on an extended business trip and I had missed hearing her voice. She carries her cell phone with her wherever she goes, so I decided to surprise her with a call. I dialled her number and my call was answered after the first ring. Strangely, however, the person answering was a gentleman whose voice I didn't recognize. I stammered a bit and then said, "I'm sorry, I seem to have dialled the wrong number."

"Who were you calling?" the man asked politely.

"Well, I was calling my daughter, Julia McCann," I replied.

"Is she flying to Vancouver?" he continued.

"Why yes, she is," I answered, becoming quite curious.

"Do you know which airline she's on?"

"Well, as far as I know, she is on Air Canada."

"Please hold on a minute," he said, and as I listened I heard, in the background, "Paging passenger Julia McCann. Please come to the Air Canada desk at Gate 5."

"Mrs. McCann," he said, now back on the phone with me, "this cell phone was found on a seat in the waiting room and was turned in here at our desk. We didn't know whose phone it was, but it seems that you have solved the mystery with your call. And—here's Julia now."

"Hi, Mom, you wouldn't believe it but. . . ."

Friday February 27

I like this thought from singer Jimmy Buffet:

Searching is half the fun: Life is much more manageable when thought of as a scavenger hunt as opposed to a surprise party.

Saturday February 28

Sometimes you have to get to know someone really well to realize you're really strangers.

Mary Tyler Moore

Sunday February 29

First Sunday in Lent

O Lord, who for our sake didst fast 40 days and forty nights: Give us grace to use such abstinence, that, our flesh being subdued to the Spirit, we may ever obey thy godly motions in righteousness and thru holiness, to thy honour and glory; who livest and reignest with the Father and the Holy Spirit, one God, world without end.

Amen

From The Book of Common Prayer

March

Monday March 1

Although it is not a well-known fact, this is an important date in American history.

The Peace Corps, brainchild of President John F. Kennedy, was founded on this date in 1961. Unlike other American help abroad, the Corps does not provide a flow of supplies to poorer nations. Instead it is made up of people helping people—volunteers going abroad to share their know-how by working side by side with the native farmers, doctors and teachers.

Since its inception in 1961, more than 168,000 volunteers have spent two years (plus three months of training) of their lives helping people in less fortunate areas of the world.

The world has changed since John F. Kennedy founded the Corps. Although many volunteers still live and work in rural villages and haul their drinking water from a nearby river, it is now just as common to find a volunteer giving computer training to university staff in a city and going home at night to electricity and running water.

Currently about 7,000 volunteers, ranging in age from 18 to 65, are serving in 78 countries around the world. It is a chance to participate in a professional and cultural exchange that can have life-long educational benefits for all parties involved.

What a fine legacy for President Kennedy.

Tuesday March 2

If you are going to be able to look back on something and laugh about it, you might as well laugh about it now.

Marie Osmond

This thought came to mind in our house today as Bruce suffered an embarrassing (but funny—later) incident at suppertime.

Bruce and Marg were having company for dinner and all things were going well. Marg had made some of her specialties: spaghetti with homemade meatballs, Caesar salad and garlic bread. The spaghetti was in a large bowl with a substantial amount of tomato sauce and meatballs covering the pasta.

As Bruce went to pass the pasta to Jim, his hand slipped on the bowl, tipping it slightly. Several of the meatballs rolled off the spaghetti across the table and towards Jim's lap. Jim attempted to catch the meatballs but they were very hot so instead he tossed them in the air while rising from his chair in an effort to prevent the meatballs from hitting his trousers.

One of the tossed meatballs landed in a water glass, which then tipped over, soaking the bread and serving basket. As Bruce reached for the tipped glass, he accidentally pushed the salad bowl off the table and it landed upside down on the carpet.

As Bruce explained, "It looked like an Abbott and Costello comedy. I could hardly believe it myself. Happily we all laughed about it—and ordered in a pizza!"

Wednesday March 3

Before I got married, I had six theories about bringing up children. Now I have six children and no theories.

John Wilmot

Thursday March 4

Live your life while you have it. Life is a splendid gift. There is nothing small in it. For the greatest things grow by God's Law out of the smallest. But to live your life you must discipline it. You must not fritter it away in "fair purpose, erring act, inconsistent will," but make your thoughts, your words, your acts, all work to the same end and that end, not self but God.

This is what we call character.

Florence Nightingale

Friday March 5

Author A.A. Milne, creator of Winnie the Pooh, expressed some very wise thoughts in his works. Written for children, his books have some good advice for adults as well:

In all your thoughts, and in all your acts, in every hope and in every fear, when you soar to the skies and when you fall to the ground, always you are holding the other person's hand.

Saturday March 6

Being a grandmother and great-grandmother has been one of the greatest joys of my life. Seeing the child of your child is a feeling that could never be explained in words.

When George and I first saw our grandson it seemed nothing short of miraculous. I wanted to stand at the nursery window and look at him for hours—I never wanted to leave that window. Even after the nurse returned him to his bassinet, I continued to stare . . . child of my child. A miracle!

The joy of becoming a mother was a prelude to the joy of becoming a grandmother.

Vera Allen-Smith

If I'd known grandchildren were going to be so much fun, I'd have had them first.

Grandparents should be one of a child's most valuable resources. They should be gentle teachers of the way life was and the way it should be.

John Rosemond

Just about the time a woman thinks her work is done, she becomes a grandmother.

E.H. Dreschnack

Grandchildren are a renewal of life, a little bit of us going into the future.

Sunday March 7

Second Sunday in Lent

Here is a brief meditation based on Psalm 63, for the second Sunday in Lent.

Eternal God, our hearts are restless until they rest in you. Let your glory shine on us, that our lives may proclaim your goodness, our work give you honour, and our voices praise you forever, for the sake of Jesus Christ our Lord.

Amen

Book of Alternative Service

Monday March 8

Today is my son-in-law's birthday. Bruce enjoys his birthday, perhaps more than most, because of a tradition that started a number of years ago. At that time, Marg was having a small get-together to celebrate the occasion. The invitations were sent with a note added, "Please—no gifts."

Strangely, each guest that arrived came bearing a beautifully wrapped box, seemingly having ignored Marg's "no gifts" request.

When all the guests had arrived, John Mason, a close friend of Bruce's, explained:

"We knew that you really meant what you said when you asked us not to bring presents. However, we wanted to do something special so we brought gifts that would be appropriate for nursing home residents. We are going to deliver these gifts in your name to the Manor so that others can enjoy your birthday as well."

Happily, Bruce's friends continue this yearly ritual.

Tuesday March 9

It is the first mild day of March:
Each minute sweeter than before,
The redbreast sings from the tall larch
That stands beside our door.

There is a blessing in the air,
Which seems a sense of joy to yield
To the bare trees, and mountains bare,
And grass in the green field.

William Wordsworth

Wednesday March 10

There are two things that people worry about most these days: one, that things may never get back to normal; and the other, that they have already.

Thursday March 11

My friend Emily winters in Florida and she and her friends often eat out at a small seafood restaurant on the pier. When I asked Emily about this favourite haunt, she made me laugh with her description.

"I think the sign on the wall says it best, Edna. 'If our food or service aren't up to your standards, please lower your standards.'"

Friday March 12

Members of the Hindu faith have two celebrations to enjoy at this time of year, one religious and one a spring festival.

Mahashivaratri is celebrated as the Night of the Great Lord Shiva, one of the major deities to whom Hindus direct their devotion.

The night before the feast, four worship ceremonies, or pujas, are held. Texts are recited, songs are sung and stories are told before the 24-hour fasting period ends with a great feast.

Holi is one of the most boisterous and exuberant Hindu festivals, during which men and women and children smear each other with coloured powder (gulal) and throw coloured water on each other.

The Holi festival is a day when good triumphs over evil, light vanquishes darkness, and the earth gives birth to a brand-new cycle of growth.

Although Holi has roots deep in ancient Hindu mythology, this joyous festival is now celebrated by people of different faiths.

Canadian Hindus celebrate Holi with dancing, singing and feasting.

Saturday March 13

The deeper man goes into life, the deeper is his conviction that this life is not all; it is an "unfinished symphony." A day may round out an insect's life, and a bird or a beast needs no tomorrow. Not so with him who knows that he is related to God and has felt the power of an endless life.

Henry Ward Beecher

Sunday March 14

Third Sunday in Lent

We beseech thee, Almighty God, look upon the hearty desires of thy humble servants, and stretch forth the right hand of thy Majesty, to be our defence against all our enemies; through Jesus Christ, our Lord.

Amen

A Collect from The Book of Common Prayer

Monday March 15

Not for a single day
Can I discern my way,
But this I surely know—
Who gives the day
Will show the way,
So I securely go.

John Oxenham

Tuesday March 16

Imagine if you succeeded in making the world a perfect place for your children, what a shock the rest of life would be for them.

Joyce Maynard

Wednesday March 17

For all of my readers who are of Irish descent (and for those who would like to claim an Irish heritage) may I wish you a happy St. Patrick Day.

This very old rune was said to have been spoken by St. Patrick on his way to Tara.

I arise today . . . . . .
Through the strength of heaven:
Light of the sun,
Radiance of the moon,
Splendor of fire
Speed of lightning,
Swiftness of wind,

Depth of sea,
Stability of earth
Firmness of rock.

Thursday March 18

Faith is not belief without proof: it is trust without reservation.

Martin Hulsemann

Friday March 19

My granddaughter Phyllis and her husband, Bill, have close friends of the Jewish faith. Each year at this time, they and their twins, Justin and Jenny, have enjoyed celebrating the Feast of Lots, known as Purim, with the Rosenbaum family. Purim is the last festival before Passover.

The story of Purim is found in the book of Esther. It describes the escape of the Persin Jews from a massacre planned by Haman, minister to the King. The massacre was averted when Queen Esther overheard Haman's plan to kill all the Jews in the kingdom. Using a purim, a kind of die, he had cast lots for the date for his plan. With Ether's help, the Jews were well-armed and prepared to defend themselves. The next day they celebrated their victory over Haman.

Although Jenny and Justin are away at university this year, Purim was always one of their favourite times with their friends.

Purim is a preferred festival among Jewish

children. Usually the Megillah (the scroll of Esther) is read aloud. Each child has a noise-maker called a gregger, and each time that the name Haman occurs in the story, the children drown out his name by shaking a gregger or by hissing and booing.

Purim is a time when money is given to the poor and gifts of baked foods and fruit are exchanged.

It is a happy time in Jewish homes.

Saturday March 20

A favourite Purim treat is a three-cornered filled pastry called a Hamantaschen. The cookies are said to represent Haman's three cornered hat.

Hamantaschen Cookies

1 stick (4 oz./125 g) unsalted butter, softened
2 tbsp. (30 mL) confectioner's sugar
2 egg yolks
3 tbsp. (45 mL) ice water
1 1/2 cups (375 mL) flour
butter (to grease the cookie sheet)
apricot jam

1. Cream the softened butter and sugar together in a large bowl. Add the egg yolks and continue to blend well.
2. Add the ice water. Gradually stir in the flour

until a ball of dough is formed. Wrap the dough in plastic wrap and refrigerate overnight.

3. The next day, remove the dough from the refrigerator.
4. Pre-heat the oven to 350°F (180°C).
5. Grease a cookie sheet with butter.
6. Roll out the dough on a clean, lightly floured surface to 1/4" thickness. Using a glass (or a round cookie cutter) about 3 inches (7.5 cm) in diameter, press out cookies.
7. Place a spoonful of jam in the centre of each circle. Make a three-cornered shape by bringing three sides together, and pinching them.
8. Place the Hamantaschen about 1 inch (2.5 cm) apart on the greased cookie sheet and bake until lightly browned along the edges.

Makes 12 to 15 cookies.

Other popular fillings are poppy seeds with honey and almonds, prune jam, honey, raisins, nuts or prune filling.

Sunday March 21

Fourth Sunday in Lent

Grant, we beseech thee Almighty God, that we, who for our evil deeds do worthily deserve to be punished, by the comfort of thy grace may mercifully be relieved; through Jesus Christ our Lord and Saviour.

Amen

From The Book of Common Prayer

Monday March 22

Yesterday, the first day of spring, is a double celebration in our family.

Spring! The time of renewal, the beginning of new life is also the birthday of my great-grand-daughter Bethany. A child with a sunny disposition, she brings spring into any room that she enters. For her and for our new season, I offer these lines:

All the birds have come again,
Hear the happy chorus!
Robin, bluebird, on the wing,
Thrush and wren this message bring.
Spring will soon come marching in,
Come with joyous singing.

Tuesday March 23

Robert Benchley passed away in 1945, but stories about this man live on.

Once, when he was younger, he was visiting at the estate of a very elderly, boring maiden aunt.

The dear old lady had planned to go for a walk with him after tea one afternoon, but Benchley excused himself on account of bad weather.

Some time later his aunt found him going out the back door alone.

"Oh, Robert," she called, "has it cleared up?"

"Only partly," was Benchley's reply. "Enough for one but not enough for two," and he left . . . . alone.

Wednesday March 24

I must confess that I find smoking an abhorrent vice. Too often smokers are careless with the ashes or the butts, and there always seems to be a stale smoke odour about the homes of smokers.

I am thankful that all restaurants in our area have now banned smoking, but before the ban went into effect, our favourite restaurant had posted this sign.

"If you want to put your ashes and cigarette butts in your cup and saucer, let the waitress know and she will serve your coffee in an ash-tray."

Thursday March 25

My friends and I were talking the other day, as we often do, about our grandchildren. My friend Mildred expressed concern about one of her great-grandchildren, whom she feels is somewhat overweight.

Thanks to too much high-fat fast food and a lack of exercise, obesity has become the number one health risk facing children today.

According to experts, more than 15 percent of children are seriously overweight, leading to serious medical consequences. I was surprised to learn that a growing number of obese children are developing type 2 diabetes (usually associated with adults). Children with this disease are at greater risk for heart disease, kidney disease or stroke in later life.

What can we as parents and grandparents do to help alleviate this problem?

One of the biggest changes in lifestyle from 50 years ago is that children (and adults) are much less active. We don't walk, we drive; we watch television or work at the computer for hours in a day. Regular physical activity is essential. A walk or a bike ride as a family activity will get everyone moving and let children know that we adults feel that exercise is important in our life.

Meals prepared at home are often much healthier than those eaten out. Following the government's health guide and serving fruits and vegetables regularly will also fight high calorie consumption.

By setting a good example of eating right and exercising more, I hope that we can help all our families to a healthier lifestyle.

Friday March 26

We should so live and labour in our time that what came to us as seed may go to the next generation as blossom, and that which came to us as blossom, may go to them as fruit.

Henry Ward Beecher

Saturday March 27

The heart that is truly happy never grows old. We don't cease playing because we have grown old; we grow old because we have ceased playing.

Sunday March 28

Fifth Sunday in Lent

We beseech thee, Almighty God, mercifully to look upon thy people; that by thy great goodness they may be governed and preserved evermore, both in body and soul; through Jesus Christ our Lord.

Amen

From The Book of Common Prayer

Monday March 29

My friends Will and Muriel recently returned from a two-week trip to Italy where they visited a number of art galleries and ancient churches.

According to Will, their tour guide was a wonderfully interesting young man whose stories of the artists caught everyone's imagination.

One of the anecdotes I found very interesting

concerned Leonardo da Vinci and one of his most famous paintings.

When da Vinci was working on his painting "The Last Supper," he became angry with a certain man. Losing his temper, he lashed the other fellow with bitter words and threats. Returning to his canvas, he attempted to work on the face of Jesus, but was unable to do so. He was so upset, he could not compose himself for the painstaking work. Finally he put down his tools and sought out the man and asked his forgiveness. The man accepted his apology and da Vinci was able to return to his workshop and finish painting the face of Jesus.

Tuesday March 30

If you have built castles in the air, your work need not be lost; that is where they should be built. Now put foundations under them.

Henry David Thoreau

Wednesday March 31

When Springtime Comes to Earth
Although winter is delightful
And has its share of worth,
My pulse begins to quicken
When springtime comes to earth.

The brooks and streams and rivers
That have lain so quietly,
Now shed their icy coating
And frolic happily.

The wind becomes more tolerant
And sun seems warmer too;
Bright colours dot the landscape
As early flowers break through.

As trees bring forth their foliage
And the grass takes on its green,
One cannot help but marvel
At the panoramic scene.

So I am always grateful
When winter's lost its sting,
And nature starts unfolding
The enchanting, lovely spring.

My thanks to the unknown author.

April

Thursday April 1

Bruce came home from work today with a delightful surprise for Marg and me. While in the city, he stopped by the market and picked up several baskets of tulips and daffodils.

A number of the plants are in bloom but many more are yet to open. I'm sure they'll be beautiful for weeks! The nicest thing is that when we have enjoyed the flowers indoors, we can transplant the bulbs to our garden and enjoy them again next spring and for many springs to come.

I am so thankful for this beautiful gift of spring—and for a son-in-law who is so thoughtful.

Friday April 2

The roofs are shining from the rain
The sparrows twitter as they fly,
And with a little windy April grace
The little clouds go by.

Yet the back yards are bare and brown,
With only one unchanging tree—

I could not be so sure of spring
Save that it sings in me.

Sara Teasdale

Saturday April 3

I have always been an admirer of the poetry of Edna St. Vincent Millay. In all that I have read about this talented woman, she credits much of her success to the love and encouragement she received from her beloved mother. She once told her mother, "I am all the time talking about you and bragging, to one person or another. I am like the Ancient Mariner, who had a tale in his heart he must unfold to all. I am always button-holing somebody and saying, 'Someday you must meet my mother!'"

Sunday April 4

Palm Sunday

Ride on! Ride on in majesty!
Hark! All the tribes hosanna cry;
O Saviour meek, pursue thy road
With palms and tattered garments strowed.

Ride on! Ride on in majesty!
In lowly pomp ride on to die;
Bow thy meek head to mortal pain;
Then take, O Lord, thy power, and reign.

Dean H.H. Milman

Monday April 5

As is often the case at this time of year, Marg and I decided to begin our spring cleaning.

Isn't it amazing how things accumulate? Each time I go through this ritual I'm amazed that somehow I've got boxes of items to get rid of. How does it happen? Last spring I went through everything that I own and kept only those things that I use regularly—or so I thought! This year I find I have packed up just as many boxes of things that can go to the Salvation Army.

One nice thing about this exercise is that occasionally I will find some little treasures that I had forgotten about. Today I found a small box of photos from many years ago. A number of the pictures were taken on summer vacations when the girls were young. Seeing my handsome young

husband and my beautiful daughters at the old cottage that we rented brought a flood of memories. Recollections of the raft that we made from old barrels and scrap wood, the picnics that we took on Big Rock Island, the jars of fireflies that the girls collected, came rushing back as if it were yesterday.

I guess that if one has to do spring cleaning, the nicest part of the task is the walk down memory lane that goes with it.

Tuesday April 6

Although many festivals celebrate spring as a time of renewal and new life, the Chinese choose this time to remember friends and family members who have died.

Ch'ing Ming, a spring festival, is a day to visit the graves of ancestors. For three days before Ch'ing Ming, no hot food is eaten and no fires may be lit. On the day itself, family members tidy the burial sites, plant flowers and offer gifts of food and wine, clothing and furniture.

In the Chinese tradition, when a person dies, his or her spirit lives on. If the spirits are unhappy, they will cause trouble for those still living. For this reason, burial sites are carefully chosen and family members are buried close to one another.

Ch'ing Ming has many interesting traditions.

After the gravesites have been swept clean, a

meal is eaten at the graveside. Before the meal begins, tea or wine is poured on the ground around the grave to soothe the spirits. As well, a portion of the food from the meal is set aside for the departed souls. After the meal, a ceremony is often held where pieces of paper representing money, clothing and furniture are burned in the hope that the "spirit" of the offerings will reach to dead ancestors.

After this ceremony many families spend the rest of the day flying kites. When evening comes, small lights are placed inside the large kites to make them glow as they twist their wild patterns in the darkening sky.

It is a very beautiful tradition.

Wednesday April 7

Nothing's so dearly treasured
as the joy that families share,
Nothing's so reassuring
as knowing others care . . . .
Nothing's like a family
and the love that's always there.

Kay Andrew

Thursday April 8

Developing the mind is important, but developing a conscience is the most precious gift parents can give their children.

John Gray

Friday April 9

Good Friday

Almighty God, we beseech Thee graciously to behold this Thy family for which our Lord Jesus Christ was contented to be betrayed and given up into the hands of wicked men, and to suffer death upon the Cross, who now liveth and reigneth with Thee and the Holy Ghost, ever one God, world without end.

Amen

From The Book of Common Prayer

Saturday April 10

Marg, Mary, Julia and I spent this afternoon at our church arranging glorious flowers for tomorrow's Easter service.

Each year, at Easter, one of our parish members generously donates many flowers so that the church looks particularly beautiful on this special day. His generosity doesn't end with his gift to the church, however. He gives as many lovely blooms to our nearby nursing home. Tomorrow, although many of the residents will be unable to attend the church service, they will have the beauty of these spring bouquets to remind them of the Saviour's rising and of our own immortality.

EASTER BONNET

Sunday April 11

Easter Sunday

Jesus said, "I am the resurrection and the life; he that believeth in me, though he were dead, yet shall he live.

"And whosoever liveth and believeth in me shall never die. Believeth thou this?"

John 11:25

Monday April 12

Doubt sees the obstacles,
Faith sees the way;
Doubt sees the blackest night,
Faith sees the day;
Doubt dreads to take a step,
Faith soars on high;
Doubt questions "Who believes?"
Faith answers, "I!"

Tuesday April 13

As my longtime readers know, Mark Twain is one of my favourite authors. I can reread his works and always find something new.

In rereading *Tom Sawyer*, I gained new insight into the ending of the popular "whitewashing the fence" episode. It made a great impact on me.

Tom said to himself that it was not such a hollow world after all. He had discovered a great law of human action, without knowing it—namely that in order to make a man or a boy covet a thing, it is only necessary to make the thing difficult to attain. If there had been a great and wise philosopher, he would now have comprehended that 'Work' is what a body is obliged to do and 'Play' consists of whatever a body is not obliged to do.

Wednesday April 14

After Easter, Marg is often looking for a use for her hard-boiled eggs. My daughter Julia came up with this rather unusual use for them in her Egg Pizza.

Egg Pizza

1 uncooked 16" (35 cm) pizza shell (one that has a raised border)

3 tbsp. (45 mL) olive oil, in total

4 eggs, hardboiled and sliced

4 tomatoes, thinly sliced

2 tsp. (10 mL) dried oregano

1 tsp. (5 mL) celery salt

1 tsp. (5 mL) black pepper

4 oz. (125 g) Mozzarella cheese, grated

1. Preheat oven to 400°F (200°C). Place pizza shell on baking sheet (greased or ungreased, according to the package directions).
2. Brush 1 tbsp. (15 mL) of oil on the pizza

crust. Arrange the sliced eggs on the oiled crust. Cover the egg slices with the tomato slices and sprinkle on the celery salt, pepper and oregano.

3. Drizzle the remaining 2 tbsp. (30 mL) of olive oil over the tomato slices and then sprinkle on the cheese.

4. Bake for about 20 minutes or until the cheese bubbles. Serve hot.

Makes 4 servings.

Thursday April 15

My friend Mavis called me from her home in Winnipeg this afternoon. She had taken a rather nasty spill on her deck and had just returned from the hospital. X-rays had shown no broken bones but she would have a number of rather ugly bruises from her fall.

All things in the world of science fascinate me, but the history of the x-ray is particularly interesting.

The technology was discovered on November 8, 1895, when Wilhelm Roentgen was experimenting with light phenomena. The first x-ray photograph was taken of Roentgen's wife's hand. He named his invention X-radiation (the X stood for unknown).

In 1900, the American Roentgen Ray Society was formed to help move the radiological profession forward. When Roentgen won the first Nobel prize in physics in 1901, his first industrially manufactured x-ray tubes were made for medical diagnostics. By 1905, many hospitals had x-ray rooms with designated physicians on staff.

In the 1960s, the invention of magnetic resonance imaging (MRI) allowed doctors to visualize abnormalities in the brain and spine.

In the mid-1980s, the computer tomography, or CT scanner, established itself as an important diagnostic tool, and the PET/CT scanner, which was developed in the late 1990s, gave radiologists a nearly perfect view of the body.

Each year the field of x-ray technology advances at a mind-boggling rate.

Friday April 16

My mother drew a distinction between achievement and success. She said that, "Achievement is the knowledge that you have studied and worked hard and done the best that is in you. Success is being praised by others, and that's nice too, but not as important or as satisfying. Always aim for achievement and forget about success."

Helen Hayes

Saturday April 17

My friend Marcia sent me this quote. It comes from the inscription on Hopkins

Memorial Steps at Williams College in Williamstown, Massachusetts, and is good advice for every one of us.

Climb high
Climb far
Your goal, the sky
Your aim, the star.

Sunday April 18

Winter is past, the rain is over and gone; the flowers appear on the earth; the time of the singing of birds is come, and the voice of the turtle is heard in our land.

Song of Solomon 2:11–12

Monday April 19

My friend Emily sent me these lovely lines from Grace Noll Crowell. I hope you'll enjoy them as much as I do.

So Many Walk . . .

God, let me find the lonely ones
Among the throng today,
And let me say the word to take
The loneliness away.
So many walk with aching hearts
Along the old highway.

So many walk with breaking hearts
And no one understands;
They find the roadway rough and steep
Across the barren lands.
God help me lighten weary eyes
And strengthen nerveless hands.

God, help me brighten dreary eyes,
And let my own grief be
A sure reminder of the grief
Of those who walk with me.
When words fail, hands fail, let me go
In silent sympathy.

Tuesday April 20

If you expect perfection from people, your whole life is a series of disappointments, grumblings and complaints. If, on the contrary, you pitch your expectations low, taking folks as the inefficient creatures which they are, you are frequently surprised by having them perform better than you had hoped.

Bruce Barton

Wednesday April 21

A number of my friends and I went out to dinner this evening, to a lovely little restaurant. The food was delicious, the ambience lovely and, even nicer, there was a trio of musicians who played background music throughout our meal. They were extremely talented and we enjoyed the evening immensely.

On the way home, we all laughed about this anecdote that Jake Frampton related.

George Bernard Shaw was having lunch in a restaurant in London one day. The orchestra played one noisy song after another without intermission.

Finally summoning the head waiter, Mr. Shaw enquired, "Does the band do requests?"

"Certainly, sir," replied the waiter.

"Excellent! Would you please ask them to play dominoes until I have finished eating?"

How much more Mr. Shaw would have enjoyed our evening!

Thursday April 22

If a task is once begun,
Never leave it till it's done.
Be the labour great or small,
Do it well or not at all.

Friday April 23

I came across a letter today that I would like to share with you. This letter was sent to a dear friend after the death of her husband and it was a wonderful comfort to her.

Dear Marion,

To you and your family, I express my deepest sympathy for the loss of such an exceptionally fine man.

Neal was a very special person to me. He guided me through the uneasiness of a new career with great skill and patience, encouraging my endeavours and always complimenting the successes. As a boss he could have been stiff and authoritarian. I will always remember his advice to me as I departed on those long business trips: not "Make sure you make all your calls"; not "I expect you to make a lot of sales on this trip"; not even "Keep your expenses down." Rather he'd say, "Be sure that you eat well"—and then he would supply me with a list of restaurants that he recommended. He was a truly exceptional man.

Even more than the kindness, having known Neal I will remember his sense of humour best. It has all been a privilege for me.

With warmest feelings
D.C.

Saturday April 24

Remember that happiness is a way of travel—not a destination.

Roy M. Goodman

Sunday April 25

Hear my cry, O God; attend unto my prayer. From the end of the earth will I cry unto thee, when my heart is overwhelmed: lead me to the rock that is higher than I. For thou hast been a shelter for me, and a strong tower from the enemy.

Psalm 61:1–3

Monday April 26

As the baseball season gets under way, my grandson Marshall delights in finding interesting but little known facts about the game.

When Ty Cobb, baseball player extraordinaire, got on first base, he had an apparently nervous habit of kicking the bag. It wasn't until he retired from the game that the secret came out. By kicking the bag hard enough, Cobb could move it a full two inches closer to second base. He figured that this improved his chances for a steal or for reaching second base safely on a teammate's hit.

It's this competitive spirit that makes a good player great.

Tuesday April 27

Don't part company with your ideals. They are anchors in a storm.

Arnold Glasgow

Wednesday April 28

In our area the robin is a delightful harbinger of spring. An interesting legend tells how the robin came to get his red breast. This is a story that appeals to children—my grandchildren enjoyed it very much.

The robin was in the stable in Bethlehem on the night when Jesus was born. The newborn baby was sleeping, warmed by a small fire, as the tiny brown-feathered bird watched from the rafters. The little bird noticed that the fire was dying. Fearing that the baby would grow cold, the bird flew down and hovered over the coals, fanning them with his wings. It was a difficult task but the flames were revived. All night, whenever the fire dimmed, the bird returned and flapped his wings, keeping the Christ Child warm. When the sun rose the little bird flew off to rest, but his friends were amazed. No longer was he a plain brown bird; he now had a blazing red breast. And that is how the robin came to have his magnificent colour.

Thursday April 29

Never tell people how to do things. Tell them what to do and they will surprise you with their ingenuity.

General G.S. Patton

Friday April 30

The palest ink is better than the best memory.

Chinese proverb

May

Saturday May 1

The May Day celebration on May 1 carries on an old pagan ceremony. Druids held their feast of Bel (or Baal of the Old Testament), and for many centuries the Irish and Scottish Highlanders called the festival Beltane or Bel's Fire, when fires were lit to honour Bel.

In Victorian times flowering boughs of hawthorn and a growing tree were set up on the village green as a Maypole. The Maypole was decorated with ribbons and the young girls of the village would dance around it. The loveliest of the girls was chosen Queen of the May, a much sought-after honour.

Here in Canada, Acadians and Quebecois collect the dew, called "L'eau de mai" on May 1 because tradition says that this water has the power to heal and beautify.

A big part of the May Day celebration in England was a dance competition of Morris dancers. To this day, Morris dancers, dressed in white shirts and pants, wear bells tied on their legs and carry large white handkerchiefs to emphasize the movements of the old and intricate English folk dances.

This dance tradition has been carried over in Canada and in many cities, including Toronto, Ottawa, London and Vancouver, the Morris teams, as they are known, gather before dawn to "dance the sun up."

Many years ago, French-Canadians used to set up the Maypole, but this tradition is now pretty much restricted to Vancouver Island, where people of British descent keep the custom alive.

Sunday May 2

Praise the Lord. Praise God in his sanctuary: praise him in the firmament of his power.

Praise him for his mighty acts: praise him according to his excellent greatness.

Psalm 150:1–2

Monday May 3

Before she was married, my granddaughter Phyllis was a schoolteacher. From time to time she would assign special projects to groups of her young students. In one particular term she allowed the children to divide themselves into working groups and select their own topics to work on.

The groups seemed to organize themselves well and Phyllis was making notes on the topics that were chosen.

When she came to Tommy and inquired as to his group's choice, he told Phyllis proudly that his group was preparing to study and report on the condition of the world.

"My heavens," said Phyllis, "isn't that a little too difficult for the fourth grade?"

"Gosh no," said Tommy, "there are five of us working on it."

Oh to have the belief in one's self that the young do.

Tuesday May 4

My son-in-law John related this anecdote to me.

After the deaths of its owners, a farm had fallen into a state of disrepair.

The farm was purchased by a young man and his family. Chris, after months of backbreaking work, had transformed the property into a place of beauty. He had repaired the roof of the barn, painted the silo, mended miles of fencing, refurbished the house, mowed the weeds and planted new crops.

One day Chris's minister stopped by and, as he surveyed the farm, remarked, "God and you have sure made a big change in this place, Chris."

Chris said that he was certainly grateful to God for his goodness. Then he added dryly, "But you should have seen this place when He was running it by Himself."

Wednesday May 5

God, give me sympathy and sense,
And help to keep my courage high;
God, give me calm and confidence,
And, please, a twinkle in my eye!

Thursday May 6

A cheerful heart and smiling face put sunshine in the darkest place.

Friday May 7

Marg and I volunteer regularly at our local school. I enjoy helping youngsters learn that reading good books can bring such joy to their lives.

One of the teachers with whom we work is a

delightful young lady who seems to have no end of bright ideas to motivate her young readers.

This week was "Dr. Seuss Week" in her classroom and the activities based on the Seuss collection of books were enjoyed each day. Red Shirt Day, then Crazy Sock Day was followed on Wednesday by Wacky Wednesday, when children were encouraged to come to school wearing their clothing backwards or inside out. On Thursday the youngsters made red and white striped hats from construction paper, à la *The Cat in the Hat* and today was *Green Eggs and Ham* day. Parents and volunteers helped to serve a breakfast to the students and—yes—the eggs were tinted a delicate shade of green.

After breakfast each child was given the opportunity to read to or be read to by the visiting parents or a volunteer.

As the teacher explained, all of Dr. Seuss's books have a message. The message behind *The Cat in the Hat* is, "Don't be afraid to try new things." From *Gertrude McFuzz* we learn "Be careful about what you wish for, and be happy with what you have."

These children are learning that reading can be fun and the more they read, the more fun it becomes.

What a wonderful lesson!

Saturday May 8

Happiness is like a butterfly which, when pursued, is always beyond our grasp, but which, quietly awaited, might alight beside us.

Nathaniel Hawthorne

Sunday May 9

Mother's Day

I thank the unknown author for these lines. I hope you will take pleasure from them on this special day to honour mothers.

What Makes a Home

A man can build a mansion
Anywhere this world about,
A man can build a palace
Richly furnish it throughout.
A man can build a mansion
Or a tiny cottage fair,
But it's not the hallowed place called "Home,"
'Til mother's dwelling there.

A man can build a mansion
With high and spacious dome,
But no man in this world can build
That precious thing called "Home."

A man can build a mansion
Carting treasures o'er the foam,

Yes a man can build the building
But a woman makes it "Home."

Monday May 10

There is a Chinese proverb that says, "The longest journey begins with a single step."

Tuesday May 11

On a lovely spring day is there anything nicer than a drive through the countryside to see the farms?

"As a work of art, I know few things more pleasing to the eye, or more capable of affording scope and gratification to a taste for the beautiful, than a well-situated, well-cultivated farm."

So said Edward Everett in Buffalo, New York, in 1857. He could have uttered these words today had he been with Marg and me on our drive in the country.

There is nothing like a farmer's field beginning to bloom that is a better reminder of the renewal of spring.

Wednesday May 12

The real proof of courtesy and restraint is to have the same ailment the other person is describing and not mention it.

Thursday May 13

My friend Bonnie sent me this poem for today. I thank the unknown author for:

This Day

This day I left the trivial things behind;
The mundane things that clutter up the way.
I went in search of precious peace of
    mind . . .
I walked the path where yellow daisies sway.

I roamed the hill that seemed to touch
    the sky;
Ventured where the shy meadowlarks nest.
I watched the fluffy cloud-ships passing by;
Found the spot where wild deer pause to rest.

I gathered buttercups along the way
And watched the trembling brook,
    seaward bound;
I rested where the sun and shadows play . . .
Food for the soul I sought and surely found.

Friday May 14

Visitors to our nation's capital in the month of May are treated to the sight of thousands of blooming tulips. A thank-you gift from the Netherlands, the tulips are a reminder of the role that Canada played in the liberation of Holland in World War II.

When Douglas Howe, a former war correspondent, returned to Holland in 1984, he said, "The liberation of Holland alone, it comes to me, may well be the most lasting and meaningful triumph in the history of Canadian Arms."

On a personal note, my cousin, Jack Northgrave, was one of "our boys" who gave his life near Nijmegen, in Holland. Those tulips have special meaning for our family.

Saturday May 15

Perseverance wins over almost any obstacle. The person who is not willing to give up without "just one more try" is sure to come out on top eventually.

Think where we would be if Thomas Edison had given up before finding a successful filament for the light bulb, or if Alexander Graham Bell had not persisted with the telephone.

When I was young I observed that nine out of every ten things I did were failures, so I did ten times more work.

George Bernard Shaw

Sunday May 16

Praise him with the sound of the trumpet: praise him with the psaltery and harp.

Praise him with the timbrel and dance: praise him with stringed instrument and organs.

Psalm 150:3–4

Monday May 17

I have a number of friends who make quilts. Susan Simpson in Ontario and Glenna Dimmig in Pennsylvania are two of my younger friends who do exquisite work—such fine stitching that my old eyes can barely appreciate their skills.

Quilting has become very popular in recent years. Somewhere over time, quilts evolved from something that provided warmth on cold nights into a form of artistic expression. They have become a way to tell stories, share ideas and convey creative thoughts.

Sue has been making quilts for many years. Whenever she travels, she searches out material at the small fabric stores and is often lucky enough to find fine fabrics for very little money. Her fabric hunts are a part of the joy Sue finds in quilting.

Glenna, who lives in the Amish area of Lancaster, Pennsylvania, was chairman of one of the largest quilt exhibits in the United States. Her hard work and dedication to this meticulous craft are something to be admired by us all.

SPRING MORNING

Tuesday May 18

As minister's wife, I was often called upon to serve afternoon tea to visiting members of our parish. At first, I was quite nervous and worried each time about the food I would serve. A dear friend offered me her recipe for cream scones and my worries were over. These delicious scones are easy to make but mouthwatering good.

Cream Scones

2 cups (500 mL) all-purpose flour
2 tsp. (10 mL) baking powder
1/8 tsp. (1/2 mL) salt
1/4 (50 mL) cup sugar
1/3 cup (75 mL) butter, cubed
1/2 cup (125 mL) whipping cream
1 large egg
1 1/2 tsp. (7 mL) vanilla extract
1 egg white
1 tsp. (5 mL) water
sugar

1. Preheat oven to 425°F (220°C). Combine first 4 ingredients. Cut in butter with a pastry blender until mixture is crumbly.
2. In a second bowl, whisk together cream, egg and vanilla; add to flour mixture, stirring just until dry ingredients are moistened.
3. Turn dough out on to a lightly floured sur-

face. Pat dough to 1/2-inch (1 cm) thickness. Cut with a 2 1/2-inch (6-cm) round cutter and place on baking sheets.

4. Whisk together egg white and 1 tsp. (5 mL) water; brush mixture over tops of scones. Sprinkle scones with additional sugar.
Bake for 13 to 15 minutes or until the scones are lightly browned.

Makes 1 dozen scones.

Served with whipped cream and strawberry jam, these scones are unbeatable!

Wednesday May 19

Visitors always give pleasure—some when they come, others when they go.

Thursday May 20

What wise words came from Anne Frank while she and her family hid from the Germans in World War II:

The best remedy for those who are afraid, lonely, or unhappy is to go outside, somewhere where they can be quite alone with the heavens, nature and God. Because only then does one feel that all is as it should be and that God wishes to see people happy amidst the simple beauty of nature.

Friday May 21

Do not pray for easy lives. Pray to be stronger men. Do not pray for tasks equal to your powers. Pray for powers equal to your tasks. Then the doing of your work shall be no miracle, but you shall be the miracle.

Phillip Brooks

Saturday May 22

This is the first long weekend of our summer season and, as has been our custom for years, we are in Muskoka.

This is such a beautiful area of Ontario and I enjoy every minute of my time spent here with Eleanor. After Eleanor's husband, Bob, passed away, she faced the daunting task of the cottage opening alone. Marg, Bruce and I were only too glad to help her with the chores. The adage "many hands make light work" certainly applies here. Bruce tackles the big chores, while Marg, Eleanor and I make ready the interior for another season.

There are any number of things to see and do here in cottage country, but one of my favourites can be done right here at Eleanor's cottage.

This evening, after we had finished our dinner, we sat on the porch and watched as the steamship *Segwun* passed by the end of the dock. This ship is the last of the original steamships of the Muskoka Lakes Navigation and Hotel Company, which served the three Muskoka lakes in the early 1900s.

In 2002, another ship, this one a replica, the *Wenonah II*, was launched from Gravenhurst and now joins the *Segwun* in daily trips on the lakes.

A voyage on either of these ships is a trip back in time to a quieter, gentler era.

We enjoy watching as they slip by, lights glowing in the early evening darkness.

Sunday May 23

Praise him upon the loud cymbals: praise him upon the high sounding cymbals.

Let every thing that hath breath praise the Lord. Praise ye the Lord.

Psalm 150:5–6

Monday May 24

Victoria Day

This is the Victoria Day holiday here in Canada. Born in 1819, Queen Victoria was just 18 years old when she took the throne after her uncle's death. She was to be the longest reigning British monarch, ruling until her death on January 21, 1901. Victoria's birthday—May 24—was made a permanent holiday and, since 1952, it has been celebrated in Canada on the Monday preceding May 24.

In many parts of Canada, it is a time to catch up on gardening, ready the cottage for summer or perhaps to do a little house or yard work.

In Newfoundland, this holiday has traditionally been the occasion of the year's first camping and trout fishing trip.

The tradition of a trouting holiday began around 1900, and has been carried on ever since. Although spring has often arrived by the 24th, there are other years when this day in May can be fog-shrouded with icy wind and harbours filled with icebergs. It takes a hardy soul to keep up this tradition.

Tuesday May 25

You must learn day by day, year by year, to broaden your horizon. The more things you love, the more you are interested in, the more you enjoy, the more you are indignant about—the more you have left when anything happens.

Ethel Barrymore

Wednesday May 26

The time you spend with your grandchildren today gives them memories that will live on forever.

Audrey Sherins and Joan Holleman

Thursday May 27

You cannot teach a child to take care of himself unless you will let him take care of himself. He will make mistakes; and out of those mistakes, will come his wisdom.

Henry Ward Beecher

Friday May 28

My grandson Marshall and his wife, Jamie, are enthusiastic sailors. In March of 2003 they were glued to the television as they watched the America's Cup races from "down under" in New Zealand. New Zealand, the defending champion, was beaten resoundingly by the yacht from Switzerland—5 to 0—bringing the sailor's biggest prize to Europe for the first time in the 152-year history of the race.

What Marshall found almost as interesting as the yacht race itself was the high-tech research that went into the design of the Swiss yacht *Alinghi*, the winner.

The Swiss Federal Institute of Technology in Lausanne, Switzerland, had 15 scientists and 20 students design the vessel and the victory was saluted as victory for sailing with science.

Patrick Aebischer, president of the institute, said that the design of the yacht combined "science, technology, materials and modelling with intuition and spirit."

The design was based on a simulation of water

flowing around *Alinghi*'s hull as well as air passing around the mast and sails.

The same principles can be used to study movement of air around airplanes and will help doctors and scientists study blood circulation and cardiovascular disease.

Who could ever have imagined that the sport of sailing could produce a medical breakthrough? We really do live in a remarkable age.

Saturday May 29

A great deal of talent is lost to the world for want of a little courage. Every day sends to their graves obscure men whose timidity prevented them from making a first effort.

Sydney Smith

Sunday May 30

Hear my cry, O God; attend unto my prayer.

From the end of the earth will I cry unto thee, when my heart is overwhelmed: lead me to the rock that is higher than I.

Psalm 61:1–2

Monday May 31

Today is Memorial Day for our American neighbours. Once a day set aside to honour those who died serving their country, it is now a time to pay tribute to all friends and relatives who have passed away.

Stepping Ashore

Oh! Think to step ashore,
And find it Heaven;
To clasp a hand outstretched,
And find it is God's hand!
To breath new air,
And that celestial air;
To feel refreshed,
And find it immortality;
Ah, think to step from storm and stress
To one unbroken calm;
To awake and find it Home.

Robert E. Selle

June

Tuesday June 1

George and I had a very happy marriage and often friends would ask the secret of our success. We didn't have any "secret formula" but our relationship was built on love, trust and sharing. We shared good times and bad and through it all we loved each other.

Time is:
Too slow for those who wait,
Too swift for those who fear,
Too long for those who grieve,
Too short for those who rejoice,
But for those who love . . .
Time is eternity.

Henry Van Dyke

On this anniversary of our marriage, I remember George with a grateful heart.

Wednesday June 2

June has traditionally been the month of weddings. My husband, George, was always very busy during the month, sometimes participating in as many as four weddings on any Saturday in June.

My son-in-law John, also a minister, stopped by today after performing a ceremony in the Chapel-on-the-Hill. He amused us with this story.

A little girl was attending a wedding for the first time. She turned to her mother and whispered, "Why is the bride's dress white, Mommy?"

Her mother, keeping the explanation simple, replied, "Well, white is the colour of happiness and this is the happiest day of her life."

The little girl sat back and reflected for a moment before again leaning forward and asking, "So then why is the groom wearing black?"

Thursday June 3

If we fill our hours with regrets over the failure of yesterday, and with worries over the problems of tomorrow, we have no today in which to be thankful.

Friday June 4

Welcome your problems. Through solving problems, we gain life's greatest satisfaction.

Saturday June 5

Bruce and Marshall returned from golfing today in their usual state of frustration. In explaining his lack of success, Marshall used the following poem. I hope you enjoy it as much as I did.

In my hand I hold a little ball,
White and dimpled, rather small.
O, how bland it does appear,
This harmless looking little sphere.

It has made me yell and cry,
I hate myself and want to die.
It promises a thing called par,
If I can hit it straight and far.

To master such a tiny ball,
Should not be very hard at all.
But my desires the ball refuses,
And does exactly as it chooses.

It hooks and slices, rolls and dies,
And disappears before my eyes.
Often it will have a whim,
To hit a tree or take a swim.

With miles of grass on which to land,
It finds a tiny patch of sand.
Then has me offering up my soul,
If only it would find the hole.

It's made me whimper like a pup,
And swear that I will give it up.
And take a drink to ease my sorrow,
Knowing . . . I'll be back tomorrow.

Author unknown

Sunday June 6

O, Holy Spirit, descend plentifully into my heart, enlighten the dark corners of this neglected dwelling and scatter there Thy cheerful beams.

St. Augustine

Monday June 7

Music has always been a large part of my life. The music of the church, of course, was most prevalent of all in our home, but my parents exposed us to many types of music.

"Big band" music is still a great favourite of mine and, on Saturday, our family attended a benefit concert featuring the Spitfire Band. What a marvellous performance!

This widely known Canadian group quickly has an audience whistling, clapping and cheering as they perform a seemingly endless supply of tunes from the 40s and 50s.

For those in my age group, it was a nostalgic revue about an irreplaceable musical era, a time to rejoice in its revival through the sounds of this extremely talented group.

Tuesday June 8

A good deed is never lost; he who sows courtesy reaps friendship; he who plants kindness gathers love.

St. Basil

Wednesday June 9

And so it comes again . . . How is it that the year seems to pass so quickly and my birthday has arrived once more?

So many people have given us wise (or amusing) thoughts on old age. Here are but a few:

Old age is like everything else; to make a success of it, you've got to start young.

It's not how old you are, but how you are old.

A woman seldom gets old enough to admit that she is old.

I'm 65 and I guess that puts me in with geriatrics, but if there were 15 months in every year, I would only be 52.

James Thurber

Thursday June 10

We have come to the time of year that my son-in-law Bruce has come to dread: pre-summer diet time.

Actually Bruce did very well over this past winter and gained very little weight. Nonetheless, he is anxious to lose those few extra pounds. As he remarked today, "My June diet is that time when the hours get longer and the portions get shorter."

Friday June 11

I was awake to see the sunrise today and I was reminded of these words from Henry David Thoreau.

Now the king of day plays bo-peep round the world's corner and every cottage window smiles a golden smile—a very picture of glee. I see the water glistening in the eye. The smothered breathing of awakening day strikes the ear with an undulating motion over hill and dale, pasture and woodland, come they to me, and I am at home in the world.

Saturday June 12

I simply love strawberries! Here in Ontario the month of June is the time to enjoy this luscious fruit. A delicious dessert is Strawberry Crumble Pie.

Crust/topping
1 cup chopped almonds [available in bulk in
   most grocery stores]
2 cups all purpose flour
1/2 cup granulated sugar
3/4 cup chilled butter, broken into small pieces

Filling
1/2 cup granulated sugar
1 1/2 tbsp. cornstarch
4 cups strawberries, sliced

1. Preheat the oven to 350°F. and roast the almond pieces until toasted [about 5–6 minutes]. Remove the nuts and increase the oven temperature to 450°F.
2. In a blender or a food processor chop the nuts until they are finely ground [about 5–6 seconds]. Watch carefully, as grinding them too long will result in nut butter . . . not what you want.
3. In a large bowl, mix together the nuts, flour and sugar. Using a pastry blender or 2 knives, cut the butter into the flour mixture to form coarse crumbs.
4. Using your fingers, press half of the crumb mixture evenly into the bottom and sides of an 8 or 9 inch tart pan or pie plate.
5. In a medium bowl, mix together the sugar and the cornstarch. Add the berries and mix thoroughly.
6. Spoon the berry mixture evenly into the crust.
7. Cover the berries with the remaining crumb mixture.
8. Bake until topping is golden and the filling is bubbling, about 30 minutes.
9. Remove from the oven and cool about 10 minutes. Serve warm with vanilla ice cream or whipped cream.

Makes 6 servings.

Sunday June 13

Then God said, "Let the earth produce fresh growth, Let there be on the earth plants bearing seed, fruit trees bearing fruit with seed according to its kind." So it was; the earth yielded fresh growth, plants bearing seed according to their kind and trees bearing fruit each with seed according to its kind, and God saw that it was very good.

Genesis 1:11–12

Monday June 14

After seeing yet another wedding group being photographed at the Mill Pond on Saturday, I was reminded of this poem from my friend Marcia.

> The bridal veil was fragile net,
> The bridal gown was lace.
> The bride wore slippers on her feet
> A smile upon her face.
> The bride wore gloves of softest silk,
> And garlands in her hair.
> The bride's bouquet was white.
> P.S. The groom was also there.

Tuesday June 15

In Canada's westernmost province, British Columbia, a double celebration occurred on the 13th of this month. On that date, in 1792,

Captain George Vancouver, leaving his ships moored in Birch Bay, rowed with his men into Bernard Inlet, where he discovered the site that now bears his name. On the same day in 1866, the small settlement that had grown up was burned right to the water's edge. The people wasted no time, however, in planning a new and even greater city. Vancouver, a city twice born, is the largest city in British Columbia and the shipping capital of western Canada.

Wednesday June 16

I enjoy the humour of Stephen Leacock, that great Canadian humorist.

Once invited to accompany a group of bird watchers on a pre-dawn expedition, he answered the invitation in his own inimitable style.

"Ladies, I regret to tell you that I am the kind of man who would have absolutely no interest in an oriole building a nest unless it built it in my hat in the checkroom at my club."

Thursday June 17

What sweetness is left in life if you take away friendship? It is like robbing the world of the sun.

Marcus Tullius Cicero

She would let the pigeons out for a flight and then, as they soared heavenward, she'd say, "Now watch."

Just as the bird dropped its wing, prior to a roll, Sarah would shout, "Roll!" as she waved her finger at the flying bird. It would perform a perfect roll and Sarah's pals would be astonished.

"How did you teach him that?" they would ask in hushed tones.

Sarah would just smile.

Wednesday June 23

Just as people lit fires in ancient times to strengthen the weakening sun at winter solstice, so too did they light "midsummer fires" to help keep the sun strong.

Later, as Christianity spread through Europe, the fires became known as St. John's Fires, heralding St. John's Day, June 24. Many European-Canadians still light midsummer fires to celebrate the solstice.

Danish-Canadians hold their celebration for St. Hans Day out in the country on the eve of the 24th. They light a huge bonfire for the burning of an effigy of a "witch," and there is singing, dancing and partying.

Polish-Canadians also light bonfires on "Sobotka" and set candlelight wreaths afloat on rivers and streams.

Latvian-Canadians celebrate St. John's Day with picnics and bonfires.

The greatest celebration of the day takes place in Quebec, where St. Jean Baptiste is honoured with festivities many and varied.

The night before, on the 23rd, there is a "Communion of Bonfires" all along the banks of the St. Lawrence River. One town begins with its fire and this is the signal for the next town or village to light its fire. The fires travel on both sides of the river, all the way to the Ontario border. Also called the "Fires of Joy," they are a part of a long-lasting custom that came to Canada with the early French-Canadian settlers.

When there was nothing more to add,
He knew his masterpiece was complete,
And so . . .
He called it . . . Dad.

Monday June 21

Another season is upon us! Summer arrived today with a great flourish of sunshine and warm weather.

The older I get, the more I look forward to those "lazy, hazy, crazy" days of summer.

Welcome . . . . Welcome . . . . Summer!

Tuesday June 22

Marg and I were walking through the park today when several pigeons landed on the bench beside us. Seeing them reminded me of a young neighbour of some years ago.

Sarah had a pigeon coop in her back yard that housed several varieties of pigeons, including the type known as rollers. That particular variety had a most peculiar habit. As one flew high in the sky, it would suddenly do a roll, similar to that of an aerobatic airplane. Just before doing the roll, its left wing did a little dip, as a forewarning.

Sarah loved to have her pigeons "perform" for her young friends, and occasionally I would be there to watch as well.

"Mrs. McCann," she would call, winking at me, "I am just showing my friends my trained pigeons."

Friday June 18

The life of every man is a diary in which he means to write one story—and writes another: and his humblest hour is when he compares the volume as it is with what he had hoped to make it.

James M. Barrie

Saturday June 19

Before we set our hearts too much upon anything, let us examine how happy are they who already possess it.

François, duc de La Rochefoucauld

Sunday June 20

Father's Day

God took the strength of a mountain,
The majesty of a tree,
The warmth of a summer sun,
The calm of a quiet sea,
The generous soul of nature,
The comforting arm of night,
The wisdom of the ages,
The power of the eagle's flight,
The joy of a morning in spring,
The faith of a mustard seed,
The patience of eternity,
The depth of a family need,
Then God combined these qualities,

Thursday June 24

The best way I know to win an argument is to start by being right.

Lord Hailsham

Friday June 25

We hope that, when the insects take over the world, they will remember with gratitude how we took them along on all our picnics.

Bill Vaughan

Saturday June 26

The children in our area finished the school year yesterday. I enjoy having the youngsters off school and hearing their joyful chatter in the neighbourhood.

Several children spent the afternoon running through the hose, keeping cool on this very hot day. I envied their energy and enthusiasm.

Someone once said, "If you want to stay young, associate with young people; if you want to feel your age, try keeping up with them."

Sunday June 27

Summer suns are glowing,
Over land and sea,
Happy light is flowing
Bountiful and free.
Everything rejoices
In the mellow rays,

All earth's thousand voices
Swell the psalms of praise.

Bishop W. Walsham How

Monday June 28

What counts is not the number of hours put in, but how much you put in the hours.

Tuesday June 29

He who has health, has hope; and he who has hope, has everything.

Arabian proverb

Wednesday June 30

Be grateful for luck, but don't depend on it.

William Feather

July

Thursday July 1

Canada Day

O ne of the most stirring patriotic songs was composed in 1867 as a song celebrating Canada's Confederation. With words and music by Alexander Muir (1830–1906) "The Maple Leaf Forever" was, for many years, the unofficial national anthem. Here, then, is a salute to Canada, our home and native land.

The Maple Leaf Forever

In days of yore,
From Britain's shore
Wolfe the dauntless hero came
And planted firm Britannia's flag
On Canada's fair domain.
Here may it wave,
Our boast, our pride
And joined in love together,
The thistle, shamrock, rose entwined
The Maple Leaf Forever.

The Maple Leaf
Our Emblem Dear,

The Maple Leaf Forever
God save our Queen and heaven bless,
The Maple Leaf Forever.

Friday July 2

As baseball season gains momentum, we are inundated with facts and figures from the game's broadcasters. My son-in-law John found this little-known fact in an old book some years ago. The "Iron Man" of baseball is, in fact, a woman. Miss Harriet Smith of Brookline, pitching for the Hollywood Girls team in 1931, pitched 83 innings in one week, and 200 games in one playing season.

Saturday July 3

We have many spectacular thunderstorms in summer, and I especially enjoy watching the "show" that lightning strikes provide.

One summer's evening, the girls and I were at a cottage on our own, awaiting George's arrival. The storm came rumbling out of nowhere and we watched as sheets of rain came down like a curtain over the cottage. The lightning was flashing and the girls were more than a little nervous when the power went out.

Not wanting them to be frightened, I pulled stools over to the window and told them that it was like a fireworks show. We perched on the chairs and "oohed" and "aahed" at every flash. It was a marvellous show . . . and a wonderful memory.

Sunday July 4

As long as the earth endures, seedtime and harvest, cold and heat, summer and winter, day and night will never cease.

Genesis 8:22

Monday July 5

Yesterday was "The Glorious Fourth," Independence Day for our American neighbours. From one side of the country to the other, the Stars and Stripes flew proudly in a patriotic display that is unrivalled, and voices joined together to sing:

Oh! say can you see,
By the dawn's early light,
What so proudly we hailed
At the twilight's last gleaming?
Whose broad stripes and bright stars,
Through the perilous fight,
O'er the ramparts we watched
Were so gallantly streaming?
And the rockets red glare,
The bombs bursting in air,
Gave proof through the night

That our flag was still there.
Oh! say does that star spangled banner yet
  wave
O'er the land of the free and the home of
  the brave?

Tuesday July 6

Summer in Canada gives us a marvellous opportunity to explore some of the naturally beautiful areas that are in each province from coast to coast. My good friend Mavis Tewbury, a native of Winnipeg, Manitoba, described to me one such area that she visited recently with her great-grandchildren. Spirit Sands, Canada's only desert, is found in Spruce Woods Provincial Heritage Park, just 30 km south of the Trans Canada Highway, near Carberry, Manitoba.

Mavis wrote, "Edna, imagine! All these years I've lived in Manitoba, and this was my first visit to the Manitoba Desert (Spirit Sands). The beautiful dunes stretch about 5 km long and about 30 metres high and they were formed about 10,000 years ago when a glacial lake, Lake Agassiz, covered southern Manitoba.

"Inaccessible until the 1960s, there's now a horse-drawn covered wagon tour that takes you to explore the desert area.

"Allison, David and I went on the 90-minute tour and it was fascinating! The wagons have padded seats for comfort and wagoneers give interesting talks along the route, describing the plants and animals of the region (many of which cannot be found anywhere else in Manitoba).

"The first stop is at Devil's Punch Bowl, a pit where underground streams have created a pond of warm blue-green water. Painted turtles abound here and white spruce rim the 'bowl.'

"The second stop is at the Spirit Sands, the dunes that are constantly shifting and re-shaping themselves according to the direction of the winds that blow the sand into ripples.

"Although somewhat remote, this is a most worthwhile and interesting part of the province to see."

Wednesday July 7

I particularly enjoy our summer's days and my happiness brought to mind this lovely poem from Grace Noll Crowell.

To Those Who Are Content

To those who are content
I lift my song—
To those who are at peace
Where they belong.

Who rise and question not,
Who go their way
Happily from dawn
To close of day;

Who labour and who earn
The bread they eat,
Who find their rest at night
Is deep and sweet;

Who ask no more of life
Than they can give,
Oh, beautifully fine
I think they live;

Who are content to serve,
To love, to pray,
Leading their simple lives
From day to day.

Thursday July 8

Summer is the time of year when a mother appreciates nothing so much as a teacher's patience.

Friday July 9

Marg, Bruce and I went to watch my great-grandson Michael's baseball game this evening. I couldn't help but laugh as Marshall quoted Earl Wilson: "For the parents of a Little Leaguer, a baseball game is simply a nervous breakdown, divided into innings." Happily, the parents of the children on Michael's team are not strongly competitive and the game remains as it should for the children—a time to have fun!

Saturday July 10

This evening we will enjoy a barbecue dinner to celebrate both Phyllis and Bill's anniversary, and Justin and Jenny's birthday. Although the actual date for both was yesterday, the twins were working last night and would have missed out on the fun had we celebrated yesterday.

It truly seems like yesterday as I think back to that day when the twins were born. Tiny babies—Jenny at three pounds and Justin at three pounds twelve ounces—they have grown into fine healthy young people whose potential seems limitless.

"You rear a child like you throw a ball," said the

country parson. "Give it the best shot you can while it's in your hands, for it must go the rest of the way by itself."

I am so proud of Phyllis and Bill. They have done a wonderful job of raising their two children. I shall celebrate this evening with a sense of love, joy, pride and a grateful heart for all the blessings that life has given me. I hope that each of you may also be so blessed.

Sunday July 11

All things bright and beautiful,
All creatures great and small,
All things wise and wonderful,
The Lord God made them all.

Monday July 12

Today Marg had a lovely luncheon for the members of her book club. Marg is a competent and organized hostess who manages to have everything ready early enough that she is able to spend time with her friends, not in the kitchen.

This afternoon the topic of conversation turned to cosmetic surgery. One of the newer techniques involves injections of the botulinum toxin Type A (Botox) that temporarily improves the appearance of facial frown lines and wrinkles.

I find the desire to look much younger than one's age a strange phenomenon. To pay a plastic surgeon thousands of dollars to accomplish this seems absurd to me.

Happily, there exists more than one kind of beauty. There is the beauty of infancy, the beauty of youth, the beauty of maturity and . . . the beauty of age.

George Augustus Sala

There is a unique quality that time gives to those of us who are older, and if we "lift" or "tuck," we take away something that is an essential part of who we are.

Perhaps my thinking is old-fashioned. In this case it will match my wrinkles!

Tuesday July 13

Keep changing. When you're through changing, you're through.

Bruce Barton

Wednesday July 14

If you don't believe in co-operation, just observe what happens to a wagon when one wheel comes off.

Thursday July 15

Something that I have come to enjoy very much is the Senior Citizen's Bus Tour that leaves weekly from our local nursing home. My friend Lila and I joined today's tour, and it was as enjoyable as ever.

Today we did a tour of the Ontario Science Centre in Toronto, followed by afternoon tea at the Old Mill, in the west end of the city.

Loneliness can be a senior's greatest enemy. Bus tours such as these provide a wonderful way to get to meet new friends.

Friday July 16

Samuel Johnson once noted that the two most engaging powers of an author are that new things are made familiar and familiar things are made new.

Saturday July 17

How nice it is to enjoy a cook-out on a warm summer's evening. My son-in-law John, not usually a culinary genius, surprised us all tonight with a barbecue salmon dinner that was delicious.

Grilled Salmon and Greens

1/2 cup (125 mL) each Balsamic vinegar and red wine vinegar

1/2 cup (125 mL) chopped packed fresh basil

1 tbsp. (15 mL) each minced garlic and fresh tarragon

2 tsp. (10 mL) Dijon mustard

1/2 cup (125 mL) light olive oil
4 boneless Atlantic Salmon fillets (6 to 7 oz./
   130 to 200 g) each)
8 to 10 cups (2 to 2.5 mL) mesclun salad mix
2 large tomatoes sliced

1. In a blender or food processor, combine vinegars, basil, garlic tarragon and Dijon mustard. With blender or processor on, slowly add olive oil. Refrigerate until ready to use (or up to 2 days).
2. Rinse fillets, pat dry and place in a 9 x 13 inch (22 x 33 cm) baking dish. Pour 3/4 cup (175 mL) of the blended vinaigrette over the fillets. Reserve remainder. Refrigerate fillets about 1 hour, turning fillets every 15 minutes.
3. Lift fillets from vinaigrette; discard marinade. Place salmon on a well-greased grill 4 to 6 inches (10 to 15 cm) above medium-hot coals. Cook about 4 minutes on each side (cut to test whether done). Remove from grill; keep warm.
4. Toss greens well with reserved vinaigrette and divide on 4 plates. Lay warm fillets over greens; garnish with tomato slices.

Makes 4 servings.

FRAGRANT BOUQUET

Sunday July 18

This is my Father's world,
And to my listening ears
All nature sings, and round me rings
The music of the spheres.
This is my Father's world.
I rest me in the thought
Of rocks and trees, of skies and seas,
His hand the wonders wrought.

Rev. Maltbie D. Babcock

Monday July 19

Far away there in the sunshine are my highest aspirations. I may not reach them, but I can look up and see their beauty, believe in them, and try to follow where they lead.

Louisa May Alcott

Tuesday July 20

Although it's hard to imagine, it was 35 years ago today that man first stepped on the moon. As astronaut Neil Armstrong stepped off the ladder and on to the moon, the human race accomplished its single greatest technological achievement of all time.

Do you remember the first words to come back to us from the moon?

"That's one small step for [a] man, one giant leap for mankind."

Wednesday July 21

The early settlers in our country needed special skills, and these skills are celebrated at the Calgary Stampede, in Calgary, Alberta.

Often called the greatest outdoor show on earth, it attracts the world's top professional cowboys, who compete for hundreds of thousands of dollars during the ten-day event.

The stampede was begun in 1912 by a young cowboy from Wyoming, Guy Weadick, who dreamed of gathering the finest crew of bronco busters and offering them enormous purses in competition. Weadick's dream has grown to become Canada's largest rodeo.

For any of you who have never seen a rodeo, you have missed a spectacular event. Until you see the cowboy's skills at such events as saddle bronc and bareback riding, steer wrestling, calf roping, bull riding or the chuck wagon race, it is difficult to imagine.

The stampede offers a variety of interesting things to see and do—agricultural and livestock exhibits, a Frontier Casino, an Indian Village and the Wild West Town of Weadickville.

A visit to the Calgary Stampede is a wonderful way to spend a summer week.

Thursday July 22

It's a funny thing about life: if you refuse to accept anything but the best, you very often get it.

W. Somerset Maugham

Friday July 23

When grace is joined with wrinkles, it is adorable. There is an unspeakable dawn in happy old age.

Victor Hugo

Saturday July 24

I saw a horse race on television today and I was reminded of this funny story that my friend Marcia sent me some years ago.

Ring Lardner, an American humorist, was a moody man who could suddenly become silent in the middle of a conversation. One night, while he was dining with a friend at a restaurant, he became lost in contemplation of a picture on the wall next to him. It was a very old print of a horse race at Saratoga at the end of the 19th century. Lardner, ignoring both his dinner and his companion, stared fixedly at the print, saying not a word. As his friend, respecting his silence, finished eating, Lardner finally spoke.

"You know," he said, "that jockey next to the rail isn't trying."

Sunday July 25

The Lord shall preserve thy going out and thy coming in from this time forth, and even for evermore.

Psalm 121:8

Monday July 26

When young, consider that one day you will be old. When old, remember that you were once young.

Tuesday July 27

This afternoon, as I was walking in our neighbourhood, I passed one home where a group of youngsters were lying on their backs in the front yard.

"Hi, Mrs. McCann," young David called out, lifting only his head to look at me.

Intrigued, I asked, "What are you and your friends doing?"

His head popped up again and he explained, "Well, do you see all those white clouds up there? We're trying to see who can pick out the most pictures from the clouds. See over there? Doesn't that look just like a horse's head?"

I agreed that it did indeed look like a horse's head.

How nice it was to see youngsters using their imaginations in the outdoors. Summer holidays are so brief.

Wednesday July 28

Marshall and Bruce had a game of golf after work today and they made their usual complaints about shots that went astray and putts that were missed. To them, and to all of you out there who also play golf, I offer these ideas on this great game:

The best thing that can be said about golf is that it is not compulsory.

Golf isn't so much a game as a passionate faith that you can hit it a mile the next time.

Golf is a five-mile walk punctuated by disappointments.

Many a golfer prefers a golf cart to a caddy because it cannot count, criticize . . . or laugh.

In primitive society, when native tribes beat the ground with clubs and yell, it is called witchcraft: in civilized society it is called golf.

Thursday July 29

Worry is interest paid on trouble before it is due.

Friday July 30

My friend Jake is a fisherman and I laughed as he read me these lines from Linda Greenlaw: "Edna, this is exactly how I feel. 'What I do is called FISHING. If it was easy, we would refer to it as CATCHING and there would be more people doing it.'"

Saturday July 31

Back in 1987 we were having a record heat wave.

On Sunday morning the minister rose to give his sermon. His face was flushed and he was dripping perspiration. As he mopped his brow, he said to those of us in the congregation: "It seems to me that if this heat doesn't make you reflect on your sins, nothing I can say will."

With that, his sermon ended and he sat down.

August

Sunday August 1

For the beauty of the earth,
For the glory of the skies,
For the love which from our birth
Over and around us lies,
Lord of all, to thee we raise
This our grateful psalm of praise.

F.S. Pierpoint

Monday August 2

This is the civic holiday in all provinces except Quebec. This holiday has no historical significance and most people simply look forward to a day off work to enjoy the beautiful summer weather.

Our capital city of Ottawa has an entertaining festival that runs through this holiday weekend. The Sparks Street Mall International Busker Festival is Canada's second-largest busker festival (second only to the event held in Halifax). Jugglers, comedians, mimes, musicians, storytellers and magicians come from all over the world to showcase their talents. Ottawa's own Junkyard Symphony, which makes music from old pots and pans—and even the kitchen sink—is

SUMMER GARDEN

a popular performer at this show. The trees, flowers, fountains, sculptures, outdoor benches and cafés, markets and boutiques of the Sparks Street Mall all make this festival appealing to the whole family, from the youngest to even the "very senior" senior.

Tuesday August 3

These are the things I prize
And hold of dearest worth:
Light of the sapphire skies,
Peace of the silent hills,
Shelter of the forests, comfort of the grass,
Music of the birds, murmur of little rills,
Shadow of clouds that swiftly pass,
And, after showers
The smell of flowers
And of the good brown earth—
And best of all, along the way,
Friendship and mirth.

Wednesday August 4

The whole secret of remaining young in spite of years, and even of grey hairs, is to cherish enthusiasm in oneself, by poetry, by contemplation, by charity—that is, in fewer words, by the maintenance of harmony in the soul. When everything is in its right place within us, we ourselves are in equilibrium with the whole work of God. Deep and grave enthusiasm for the eternal beauty and the eternal order, reason touched with emotion and a serene tenderness of heart—these surely are the foundations of wisdom.

Henri Frederic Amiel

Thursday August 5

I received a letter from my friend Emily today. Usually at this time of year she resides in Philadelphia, however, for this week she is at her condominium in Florida. She needed to get some work done in her southern home and felt that she should be there to supervise. It is extremely warm currently and I laughed as I read her explanation of "Summer in Florida."

You know you're in Florida during the summertime when:

* Hot water now comes out of both taps.
* The temperature drops below 90 degrees F and you feel a little chilly.
* You break into a sweat the minute you step outside at 7:30 a.m.
* The birds have to use potholders to pull the worms out of the ground.
* You burn your hand opening the car door.
* You learn that a seat belt buckle makes a pretty good branding iron.

Friday August 6

My good friend Will's love of gardening is evident in the wonderful vegetables that grow in his back-yard garden. He dropped in today to bring me a basket of his produce. I was the lucky recipient of some baby carrots, green and yellow beans, and some corn on the cob.

I noticed that Will had many more baskets filled to the brim. He seemed a little embarrassed when I asked him about them.

"Well, Edna, we have so many more vegetables than we could ever eat, so I thought I'd stop by some of our more elderly neighbours' homes. I'm pretty sure that most of them weren't able to plant their own gardens this year."

Will is so generous and he is always doing kind things for others. He likes to do his good works quietly and is embarrassed when people want to recognize his thoughtfulness.

The world needs more people like that!

Saturday August 7

I was always very fond of the cartoons of James Thurber. In looking through a very old magazine today, I found one of my favourites.

This one shows a picture of a woman on the telephone, and the caption reads:

"Well, if I dialed the wrong number, why did you answer the phone?"

Sunday August 8

If we walk in the light as He is in the light, we have fellowship one with another.

1 John 1:7

Monday August 9

My friend Lila and I sat in the garden this afternoon enjoying the beauty of the flowers and a frosty glass of iced tea.

I got into the habit of drinking a cup of tea every afternoon during my visit to England many years ago.

My dear friend Peggy Cay, who still lives in England, knew a great deal about growing tea, and the tea that she brewed each afternoon was just delicious.

You might be interested to know that tea was discovered in China thousands of years ago.

It was only introduced into Europe in the 17th century and, of course, into America even later.

China still ranks first in both production and consumption of tea, but Lila and I did our best this afternoon to raise Canada's level to somewhere near a record level.

If you need a refreshing summer drink, you'll find nothing better than a tall glass of iced tea.

Tuesday August 10

My husband, George, and I tried very hard to instill in our daughters a sense of purpose and determination. We hoped to show them that, even in the most difficult of circumstances, people need not be discouraged or give up.

George told the girls a wonderful story to illustrate this sense of determination. I was very pleased today when my grandson Marshall told me that he also uses this story with his daughter, Bethany. I know George would be pleased too.

There was an old blind horse living on a farm. The farmer had considered getting rid of the animal but never had the heart to do it, because of the years of faithful service the horse had given him.

One day the horse accidentally stumbled into a well. The farmer found him standing knee deep in water. There seemed to be no way of getting him out without great expense and, as both the well and the horse were no longer of use, the farmer decided to fill the well and have the horse buried with it.

He shovelled in the dirt as quickly as he could, but as the dirt poured in on him, the horse shook it off and trod it underfoot. Gradually the well filled up and the horse was able to step out and walk away into the pasture.

The moral, of course, is that no one can be kept down unless he is willing to be buried.

Wednesday August 11

As we advance in life, we acquire a keener sense of the value of time. Nothing else, indeed, seems of any consequence; and we become misers in this respect.

William Hazlitt

Thursday August 12

I hope you'll enjoy these lines from Henry Van Dyke as much as I do.

Life

Let me live my life from year to year,
With forward face and unreluctant soul;
Not hurrying to, not turning from, the goal.
Not mourning for the things that disappear
In the dim past, nor holding back in fear
From what the future veils; but with a whole
And happy heart, that pays its toll
To youth and age, and travels on with cheer.

So let the way wind up the hill or down,
O'er rough or smooth, the journey will be joy:
Still seeking what I sought when but a boy,
New friendship, high adventure, and a crown,
My heart will keep the courage of the quest,
And hope the road's last turn will be the best.

Friday August 13

The Icelandic Festival of Manitoba is a celebration of the Icelandic North American's proud tradition and heritage. "Isleningada gurunn," held each year in Gimli, is one of the oldest ethnic festivals, dating back to 1890.

Many Icelandic settlers emigrated to Canada after their homes in Iceland were destroyed by volcanic eruptions in 1875. The first festival, in 1890, was the brainchild of Jon Olafsson, editor of the Icelandic newspaper *Lögberg*, and the current celebration continues to reflect the interest in Icelandic culture.

Events include theatre programs, musical attractions such as the Gimli Folk Festival, a Tweener's Dance and a community singsong. There are also songwriting and poetry competitions. My friend Mavis, who attends this event each year, tells me that she enjoys the delicious food available in the park. Typical Icelandic food such as smoked lamb, skyr (which is like yogurt), rullupylsa (Icelandic brown bread), hangikjot and hardfiskur (an Icelandic treat of dried cod) are served by participants dressed in Native Icelandic costumes.

Mavis also enjoys taking her great-grandchildren to the parade on Monday morning (of the August long weekend), which is filled with clowns, bands, floats and "Vikings."

There are also many sporting events, including beach volleyball, a ten-mile run, a tug of war and the Seglavik Canoe Races. The highlight of the sports events is Islendingadunk, the "Viking

Challenge." Two contestants sit on a wooden pole stretched across water and smack each other with pillows until one of them falls off.

This festival is attended by Icelandic-Canadians and friends from across Canada.

Saturday August 14

Ann Landers once offered this wise advice: Know yourself. Don't accept your dog's admiration as conclusive evidence that you are wonderful.

Sunday August 15

Love divine, all loves excelling,
Joy of heaven, to earth come down,
Fix in us thy humble dwelling,
All thy faithful mercies crown.
Jesus thou art all compassion
Pure unbounded love thou art,
Visit us with thy salvation,
Enter every trembling heart.

Charles Wesley

Monday August 16

As I lay in bed this morning looking out at the lake and watching the sunrise, I marvelled at my good fortune. Here I am in Muskoka, a magnificent area of our country, visiting with someone whose friendship has been a treasure to me for many years.

Hours spent with old and cherished friends is some of the best time that we can enjoy in this lifetime.

Keep up your friendships: as we age we have more need of friends than ever before!

As Ralph Waldo Emerson said, "A friend may well be reckoned the masterpiece of nature."

Tuesday August 17

Eleanor and I spent today out on the water. Eleanor has one of the many antique boats that are so popular in this area. Her mahogany Ditchburn launch was built back in the 1920s, and much hard work has kept it in pristine condition.

The Ditchburn family immigrated to Canada in the 1860s and began building boats, originally to supply their family hotel with skiffs and small recreation boats.

As the Muskoka Lakes area became the summer haven for many well-to-do families, Ditchburn Boats produced a new type of power launch featuring speed, comfort and style that became enormously popular with the wealthy elite.

The Ditchburn Boat Company enjoyed wide renown and gained an international reputation as a builder of some of the finest launches of the time.

Unhappily, the boat-building industry was hit hard by the Great Depression, and Ditchburn was forced to reorganize and develop a line of less expensive runabouts.

Today many of the Ditchburn-built launches still reside on Muskoka lakes, and they are as much loved today as they were those many years ago, when they first rode on these waters.

Wednesday August 18

Part of the happiness of life consists not in fighting battles, but in avoiding them. A masterly retreat is, in itself, a victory.

Norman Vincent Peale

Thursday August 19

At this time of year, many American visitors come north to explore Canada's tourist areas.

Some years ago, an American friend visiting in Ontario was stopped for speeding. His explanation was captivating.

Charged with driving 72 mph he explained that since the Canadian gallon was larger than the U.S. gallon, he thought that miles might be longer in Canada. To cover 60 Canadian miles he thought that his speedometer should read at least 70 miles per hour.

The policeman explained the error and waived the usual fine.

Eleanor and I were laughing about this story

and trying to imagine the same gentleman making an effort to try to convert gallons—and miles—to kilometres.

Friday August 20

One of the most tragic things I know about human nature is that all of us tend to put off living. We dream of some magical rose garden over the horizon—instead of enjoying the roses that are blooming outside our window.

Dale Carnegie

Saturday August 21

One of the most popular of summer events here in Muskoka is the regatta, held in almost every lakeside cottage community. Eleanor and I were enthusiastic spectators at today's regatta, in the bay behind her cottage. Dozens of youngsters and their parents participated in swimming, sailing and canoeing events that left everyone exhausted but happy, and ready to enjoy the potluck barbecue dinner that the families shared.

What will your children remember? Moments spent listening, talking, playing and sharing together may be the most important times of all.

Gloria Gaither

Sunday August 22

Make me a clean heart, O God, and renew a right spirit from within me. Cast me not away from thy presence, and take not the holy spirit from me.

Psalm 51:10–11

Monday August 23

God gave man an upright countenance to survey the heavens, and to look upwards to the stars.

Ovid

Tuesday August 24

As the nights grow a little cooler, it makes me want to hold on to these summer days forever. How I love the summer time—and this song by Ron Shields:

> There's a time each year that we
> always hold dear,
> Good old summer time;
> With the birds and the trees and the
> sweet scented breezes,
> Good old summer time.
> When your days work is over then
> You are in clover,
> And life is one beautiful rhyme.
> In the good old summer time,
> In the good old summer time,
> Strolling through the shady lanes,
> With your baby mine;
> You hold her hand, she holds yours,
> And that's a very good sign,
> That she's your tootsey wootsey
> In the good old summer time.

Wednesday August 25

So live—decently, fearlessly, joyously—and don't forget that in the long run it is not the years in your life but the life in your years that counts.

Adlai Stevenson

Thursday August 26

I enjoyed these wise words from Albert Schweitzer:

I don't know what your destiny will be, but one thing I do know, the only ones among you who will be really happy are those who have sought and found how to serve.

Friday August 27

Hindu families have a very lovely celebration in August. Rakshabandhan is a festival based on an ancient legend that honours the ties between brothers and sisters.

As the legend goes, God Indra's wife tied a silk charm around his wrist in order to protect him from demons. With this safeguard, Indra was able to defeat his enemies and return to his home in the heavens.

Today, girls tie bracelets called rakhi, made of colourful silks or cotton thread, on their brothers' wrists. They also mark their foreheads with vermilion.

The bracelets, symbolizing the bond between brothers and sisters, are usually gold or other bright colours mixed with tinsel. When tied on the wrist by his sister, the rakhi obliges the brother to protect her. In return for his honour, the brother gives his sister a gift such as clothing, jewellery or money.

Young men who are not lucky enough to have a sister may be selected by a friend to wear a rakhi. He will then protect the girl as he would a sister.

Saturday August 28

Having more material things does not produce happiness. Happiness comes through striving to get the most out of what we already have.

Sunday August 29

For God sent not his Son into the world to condemn the world; but that the world through Him might be saved.

John 3:17

Monday August 30

Those who love deeply never grow old; they may die of old age, but they die young.

Pinero

Tuesday August 31

After a marvellous two-week holiday with my friend Eleanor, I am back at home again. As much as I love to visit, there is something wonderful about that place called "home."

If there's a heaven upon this earth,
A fellow knows it when
He's been away from home a week,
And then gets back again.

September

Wednesday September 1

This is such a wonderful time of the year. Our gardens are at their most beautiful and the fruits and vegetables abound. I hope you'll enjoy these lines from Georgia B. Adams as we welcome the beautiful month.

September's Basket

September's basket overflows . . .
Chrysanthemums sweep in,
In all their garden glory now
As golden sunbeams spin.

Just overhead bright golden pears
Suggest the harvest time;
From twining vine the tender grapes
So luscious and sublime!

From distant hills the forest yields
The slowly turning leaves,
The walnuts and the hickory nuts . . .
'Tis then my heart believes.

That glad September's basket spills

Anew, afresh each year,
To fill the very heart of man
With harvests of good cheer.

Thursday September 2

My daughter Mary has a wonderful touch when it comes to decorating with flowers. She always has fresh new ways to use the flowers that she grows, and I'd like to share with you just one of her ideas for fall decorating.

In the autumn months Mary likes to bring some of the beauty of the outdoors inside. This is done with her "basket garden."

You will need a basket with a handle, and it's wise to take the basket with you so you'll know how many plants to purchase. Select a mix of plants in 3- and 4-inch (7.5- and 10-cm) pots with different leaf sizes and shapes and include at least one tall plant and several that will cascade over the edge of the basket. Fresh-cut flowers may be added for special occasions.

1. Line the inside of the basket with foil.
2. Place the tallest plant next to the basket handle.
3. Arrange the rest of the plants so that they step down gradually in height. Mary's suggestion: Remove several plants from their pots and place them in plastic sandwich bags before arranging in the basket. Moisture-

loving plants such as ferns or creeping vines flourish in the bags.

4. Place trailing plants along the edges of the basket.

5. Cover any visible pots or plastic bags with dried moss.

6. Use a turkey baster to water pots or plastic bags.

To add fresh flowers, cut the stems to the desired length. Place each flower in a florist's vial filled with water and then push each vial into the soil of the potted or bagged plants. Clustered blooms look especially nice.

Check the florist's vials every day and add water as needed.

Fresh-cut flowers should last from a few days to a few weeks, but the houseplants will last for a few months.

Friday September 3

We should all be in the habit of expressing our appreciation. It is the essence of graciousness, kindness and fair dealing. Luckily it is also a habit that can be formed by anyone who will take the trouble.

Saturday September 4

This is the last long weekend before school starts and many families will be doing last-minute shopping for supplies as their children begin another year.

My grandson Marshall and his wife, Jamie, took their two children to the mall today. Isn't it a marvel how two children of the same parents can be so different? Bethany likes to visit every store and see what's available before she'll consent to any purchases. Michael, on the other hand, prefers the "in and out—let's get this over with" approach to shopping.

I guess it's these differences that make each one of us unique—and the world a special place.

Sunday September 5

A cheerful look brings joy to the heart, and good news to the bones.

Proverbs 15:30

Monday September 6

Labour Day

Today is Labour Day and it is my wish that each of us may know what it is to have worked hard and enjoyed some success, no matter how limited we may be. I feel that these thoughts from M.D. Babcock are especially appropriate on this Labour Day.

Opportunities do not come with their values stamped upon them. Everyone must be challenged. A day dawns, quite like other days; in it a single hour becomes quite like other hours; but in that day and in that hour the chance of a lifetime faces us. To face every opportunity of life thoughtfully, and ask its meaning bravely and earnestly, is the only way to meet the supreme opportunities when they come, whether open-faced or disguised.

Tuesday September 7

On this first day of the school year, I offer this little gem: some school children excel in social adjustment, activity participation, and initiative, while others learn to read and write.

Wednesday September 8

My granddaughter Phyllis used to be a schoolteacher. She found this copy of a teacher's contract from 1923.

The Board of Education agrees to pay Miss . . . . the sum of seventy-five dollars per month.

Miss . . . . agrees:
1. Not to get married. This contract becomes null and void immediately if the teacher marries.
2. Not to keep the company of men.
3. To be home between the hours of 8 p.m. and 6 a.m. unless she is at a school function.

4. Not to loiter downtown at any time.
5. Not to leave town at any time without permission of the chairman of the Board of Education.
6. Not to smoke cigarettes. This contract becomes null and void immediately if the teacher is found smoking.
7. Not to drink beer, wine or whiskey. The contract is null and void immediately if the teacher is found drinking same.
8. Not to ride in a carriage or automobile with any man except her brother or father.
9. Not to dress in bright colours.
10. Not to dye her hair.
11. To wear at least two petticoats.
12. Not to wear dresses more than two inches above the ankle.
13. Not to use face powder, mascara or paint the lips.
14. To keep the classroom clean: to sweep the classroom floor at least once daily; to scrub the classroom floor once a week with hot water and soap; to clean the blackboards at least once daily; to start the fire at 7 a.m. so that the room will be warm at 8 a.m. when the children arrive; to carry out the ashes at least once daily.

My goodness, haven't we come a long way since then?

Thursday September 9

Let me grow lovely, growing old—
So many fine things to do:
Lace and ivory and gold
And silks need not be new.
There is healing in old trees,
Old streets a glamour hold.
Why may not I, as well as these,
Grow lovely, growing old?

Friday September 10

Not many of us are material for greatness, according to the general acceptance of the term, but each has something to give to justify the gift of life. The humblest can become kindly and easy to live with.

I saw this framed and hanging on a wall in my doctor's office, and thought it worth remembering.

Saturday September 11

Today is the anniversary of the 2001 terrorist attacks on the World Trade Center in New York. So many people died in this tragedy, and for all those who lost friends or loved ones I offer these words of comfort from Helen Lowrie Marshall.

This I know

Grief has its rhythm—first the wild,
Swift tide of dark despair;

The time of bleak aloneness,
When even God's not there.

And then the slow receding
Till quiet calms the sea,
And bare, washed sand is everywhere
Where castles used to be.

The gentle lapping of the waves
Upon the shore—and then
The pearl-lined shells of memories
To help us smile again.

Sunday September 12

And he said unto Jesus, Lord, remember me when Thou comest into Thy kingdom. And Jesus said unto him, Verily I say unto thee, Today shalt thou be with Me in paradise.

Luke 23:42–43

Monday September 13

Remember this: it's more important to know where you are going than to see how fast you can get there.

Tuesday September 14

This morning I went for my usual walk and because it was such a beautiful day, I walked longer and farther than usual. As I strolled along, I could tell that a number of our neighbours were reaping the fruits of their gardening labours.

Home after home that I passed gave the aroma of pickling spice and tomato sauce, of onions and cucumbers, making my trek an olfactory delight.

It's a pleasant surprise for me to know that there are still many homes in which canning and preserving have not been left only to commercial enterprises.

Wednesday September 15

Let us be thankful that there still is sunshine, that we can still glimpse the blue of the sky and in our onward way, continue to look up. Let us be thankful for friends with kindly smiles and cheerful words. This time of year gives us so much for which to be grateful.

Thursday September 16

As we get older, it is often difficult to get enough exercise. I have always found walking to be a pleasant way for me to keep active and have noticed that I seem to have additional energy when I stay active. Doctors suggest that when you are more active, you'll see improved concentration and alertness; more energy and stamina; less stress, depression and boredom; more restful sleep; increased circulation; better muscle tone, strength and endurance; and easier weight control and improved appearance. (Quite an impressive list of benefits, isn't it?)

Along with walking, one of the best exercises for seniors, or any less active adults, is water aerobics. Gentle on the joints, water fitness still provides cardiovascular conditioning and muscle toning.

Our fitness centre keeps the water in the pool at a very comfortable temperature and the warm water is soothing on those arthritic joints.

If you find walking difficult and need a little extra daily activity, swimming or water aerobics are wonderful alternatives.

Friday September 17

No race can prosper till it learns that there is as much dignity in tilling a field as in writing a poem.

Booker T. Washington

Saturday September 18

Chilean-Canadians commemorate the independence of their country with a pena, or party. They sing and dance and enjoy such special food as empanadas (meat pastries with an egg and olive filling) and chichi (a drink much like cider).

Many Chileans came to Canada after the overthrow of Salvador Allende's Marxist government in 1973. Coincidentally, Allende was elected president on this same date, September 18, 1970.

Mid-September is also a time when many Spanish-speaking countries celebrate their national holidays. Canadians from Costa Rica, El Salvador, Guatemala, Honduras, Nicaragua and Mexico join together for a huge Hispanic festival. Held at the C.N.E. grounds in Toronto, it offers much to enjoy—delicious foods from every region, music, native dancing and, for the children, piñatas. It's a wonderful party!

Sunday September 19

O Lord, support us all the day long, until the shadows lengthen and the evening comes, and the world is hushed. Then in Thy mercy grant us a safe lodging and a holy rest and peace at last.

From The Book of Common Prayer

Monday September 20

Jenny and Justin are back at university and enjoying the many activities that are such a wonderful part of the university experience. Jenny was invited to a potluck dinner at the home of one of her professors. She called home to Phyllis to get a recipe for apple fritters, a favourite fall treat in our family.

Apple Fritters

4 cooking apples
juice from 1 lemon

1/4 (50 mL) cup sugar
few drops of vanilla extract
a pinch each of cinnamon, ground cardamom
    and cloves
1/2 (125 mL) cup all-purpose flour
2 eggs
1/2 tsp. (2mL) salt
5 tbsp. (75 mL) currants
oil for deep frying

1. Peel and core the apples and cut into thick rings. Place in a flat dish and sprinkle with lemon juice, 3 tbsp. (45 mL) of the sugar, the vanilla extract and spices.
2. Mix all but 2 tbsp. (30 mL) of the flour with 1 1/4 (300 mL) cups of water, stirring until batter is smooth. Add eggs, salt and remaining sugar and currants.
3. Heat the oil in a deep fryer to 350°F (180°C) (or in a heavy skillet so the oil is deep enough to cover the slices of apple). Sprinkle the remaining flour over both sides of the apple slices.
4. Using a fork, dip the apple slices into the batter. Fry in the oil until golden. Drain on paper towels. Serve with a sprinkle of confectioner's sugar or vanilla ice cream.

Makes 4 servings.

Tuesday September 21

I welcome autumn today with these lines from Robert Louis Stevenson.

Autumn Fires

In the other gardens
And all up the vale,
From the autumn bonfires
See the smoke trail!

Pleasant summer over
And all the summer flowers,
The red fire blazes,
The grey smoke towers.

Sing a song of seasons!
Something bright in all!
Flowers in the summer,
Fires in the fall.

Wednesday September 22

This is maturity:

To be able to stick with a job until it is finished; to be able to bear an injustice without getting even; to be able to carry money without spending it; and to do one's duty without being supervised.

Thursday September 23

Experience is what makes you wonder how it got a reputation for being the best teacher.

DADDY'S HELPER

Friday September 24

Autumn has arrived. Isn't it amazing how quickly the leaves have started to turn lovely shades of red and gold?

Although I hate to see the end of summer, the beauty of autumn does, in some measure, make up for the loss of the warm weather.

> Autumn with its clear, crisp air
> and sunsets of coppery hue,
> Has gently pushed away summer
> to linger till winter is due.

Saturday September 25

My nephew Peter has always loved Coca-Cola. From an early age he always chose Coke to drink with any snack: peanuts, popcorn, pizza, apples—all were washed down with his favourite drink—Coke.

My friend Jake gave me this list of uses for Coke. I'm sure Peter (and the rest of you Coca-Cola lovers) will get a kick out of it.

1. To clean a toilet: pour a can of Coca-Cola into the bowl and let it sit for one hour, then flush clean. The citric acid in Coke removes stains from vitreous china.
2. To remove rust spots from chrome car bumpers: rub the bumper with a piece of aluminum foil dipped in Coca-Cola.

3. Coca-Cola will clean road haze from your car's windshield.
4. To bake a moist ham, empty a can of Coca-Cola into the baking pan. Wrap the ham in aluminum foil and bake. Thirty minutes before the ham is finished, remove the foil and allow the drippings to mix with the Coke for a sumptuous brown gravy.

Sunday September 26

Remember the Sabbath day, to keep it holy. Six days shalt thou labour, and do all thy work: But the seventh day is the Sabbath of the Lord thy God.

Exodus 20:8–10

Monday September 27

Oh, grand chrysanthemum!
You brighten autumn days
Your golden faces brighten yards
And chase the gloom away.

N.G. Gates

Tuesday September 28

I like this thought:

Happiness is good.
The place to be happy is here.
The time to be happy is now.
The way to be happy is to make others happy.

Wednesday September 29

Do not wish to be anything but what you are, and try to be that perfectly.

St. Francis de Sales

Thursday September 30

The fellow that says, "I may be wrong but . . ." does not believe there can be any such possibility.

Ken Hubbard

October

Autumn Flight

Now the wild geese are going over,
Clanking their chains on the windless sky,
Over the cornfields, over the clover,
Shouting their wild exuberant cry:
Come with us, come with us—come.

They are calling,
And I, with no answers shaped in my mouth,
Stand where the painted leaves are falling,
Watching them disappear in the south,

Disappear from my sight and hearing,
Going to who knows what far land,
Straight as an arrow, and not fearing
The journey ahead . . .

I lift my hand
Bidding them to stay their avid going
Across the wide and uncharted track,
Calling to them and yet well knowing
That only the spring will bring them back.

As I stood at the Millpond, watching the geese fly overhead, I was reminded of this lovely poem from Grace Noll Crowell. So many of our feathered friends have now begun their "autumn flight."

Saturday October 2

Marg, Bruce and I spent several hours today visiting the late-season garage sales in our area. Bruce has been a garage sale aficionado for years, and I am a keen admirer of his skill in haggling. I don't think that he has ever paid full price for anything at one of these events, while I, on the other hand, am extremely uneasy offering anything less than the asking price for fear of offending the seller.

Bruce offers a number of excellent techniques for would-be bargain hunters and I pass them along to you today.

The most important practice, according to Bruce, is to follow the 25 percent rule. Decide what you think an item would cost if it were new, and then pay no more than 25 percent of that number.

When attempting to strike a deal, speak to the seller alone. The seller will be much more willing to haggle without an audience, who also may want the same price reduction.

When you have made an offer that the seller

has refused, turn and walk away. If he says nothing more, his price is as low as it will go . . . but more likely he will stop you before you get away and offer a better deal. Either way you'll know the price is as low as it will go.

If you don't get the item you'd like, give the seller your name and phone number and ask him to call should the article not sell. You may still get a great deal!

Good hunting!

Sunday October 3

The souls of the righteous are in the hand of God, and there shall no torment touch them.

The Apocrypha

Monday October 4

The earth does not belong to man;
Man belongs to the earth.
This we know.
All things are connected like the
Blood which unites one family.
All things are connected.

Chief Seattle

Tuesday October 5

Jonathon Edwards, a noted 18th-century theologian and clergyman, made these five resolutions to live by. We might all do well to use them.

1. I will live with all my might while I do live.
2. I will never lose one moment of time, but will improve it in the most profitable way I possibly can.
3. I will never do anything which I should despise or think meanly of in another.
4. I will never do anything out of revenge.
5. I will never do anything which I should be afraid to do if it were the last hour of my life.

Wednesday October 6

Until a few hundred years ago, most people had only the food they produced for themselves. It is no surprise, then, that the harvest was so important, and that when the grain has been harvested, the hay stored in the barns and the fruits and vegetables canned or stored in cold cellars, it was time to have the harvest festival.

When the last sheaf was picked up and hoisted high, the "harvest shout" was raised.

Well ploughed!
Well sowed!
Well harrowed!
Well mowed!
And all safely carted to the barn
With never a load throwed!
Hip, hip, hooray!

Although machinery such as combines and harvesters have taken over much of the work, it is still the custom to get together for a harvest festival or fall fair to sample what has been produced.

A variety of harvest-time festivals are held all across Canada. In western Canada, Threshermen's Days are popular harvest festivals with much importance placed on contests based on farming skills such as grain threshing.

In the provinces on the East and West coasts, where fishing seasons usually end in October, harvest festivals are held at churches in fishing ports, and freshly caught fish and fish nets are often displayed with flowers, fruits and vegetables. It is a time for all of us to be thankful for a bountiful harvest.

Thursday October 7

A Time of Plenty

Heap high the horn of plenty
From summer's bounteous yield.
Come reap the golden harvest
From fruitful tree and field.

Make haste the treasures to gather
From a generous September.
October's bright blue weather
Soon fades to cold November.

Now the joyous time of plenty
As we fill each mow and bin
And with thankful hearts and fervent
Prayer, the harvest's gathered in.

Author unknown

Friday October 8

M y friend Muriel related this funny story to me.

"Good friends were watching television one evening when one turned to the other, and said, 'What did she say?'

"'Gosh, I don't know, I didn't hear it either.'

"'Well this is ridiculous!'" replied the friend. 'You've got to get a hearing aid!'"

Saturday October 9

W e spent this Saturday afternoon of the Thanksgiving weekend at a local apple farm. Mary and Julia needed apples to make pies for our Thanksgiving dinner, and the orchards in our area offer a wide variety of the delicious fruit.

I have an interesting story about a particular type of apple.

The sweet red apple known as the McIntosh might never have become the favourite of so many fruit lovers had it not been for love.

In 1811, the first apple named for the Dundas County farmer, John McIntosh, was picked.

Some years before, McIntosh had followed his love, Dolly Irwin, from New York State to Upper Canada, where he hoped to marry her. His family had not approved of the match and so when he found that Dolly had died just before his arrival, he was too proud to return home. Instead, he set about clearing land in Dundas County. On this property he found about 20 young apple trees, which he transplanted to a clearing close to his house. After a few years, the trees bore fruit and it was discovered that the apples were of different varieties. The trees did not thrive and soon all but one had died. The one tree that remained was hardy and produced beautiful red apples that had an excellent flavour. They became known in the area as "McIntosh Reds."

Some time later, John's son Allan learned the art of grafting and soon the family had many new fruit-bearing trees. They are still known as McIntosh and are famous worldwide.

Sunday October 10

When thou hast eaten and are full, then thou shalt bless the Lord thy God for the good land which he hath given thee.

Deuteronomy 8:10

THANKSGIVING TABLE

Monday October 11

Thanksgiving Day

Thanksgiving is probably the most family-oriented holiday next to Christmas. Our family usually gathers together at the home of my grandson Fred and his wife, June, and it is a happy time of fellowship and feasting followed by several days of "Oh my goodness, why did I eat so much?"

As my son-in-law John put it, "Eat drink and be merry, for tomorrow we diet."

Tuesday October 12

We all need recipes for leftover turkey at this time of year. My sister-in-law, Marie, gave me this delicious way to use at least some of the turkey.

Turkey Chop Suey

1/2 cup (125 mL) onion slices
2 tbsp. (30 mL) butter or margarine
2 cups (500 mL) cooked turkey, diced
1 cup (250 mL) chopped celery
1 (6 oz./160 g) can sliced water chestnuts, drained
2/3 cup (150 mL) chicken (or turkey) broth

2 tbsp. (30 mL) cornstarch
1/4 tsp. (1 mL) salt

1/4 (50 mL) cup water
2 tbsp. (30 mL) soy sauce
2 cups (500 mL) bean sprouts

4 cups (1 L) hot cooked rice
1 1/2 cup sliced almonds, toasted

1. Cook onion in butter until tender but not brown; add turkey, celery, water chestnuts, and broth. Heat to boiling.
2. Combine cornstarch, salt, water and soy sauce into the turkey mixture. Cook, stirring constantly until mixture thickens.
3. Add bean sprouts and heat through.
4. Serve over hot rice and sprinkle with toasted almonds. Pass the bottle of soy sauce if desired.

Makes 4 servings.

Wednesday October 13

We must be willing to pay a price for freedom, for no price that is ever asked for it is half the cost of doing without it.

Thursday October 14

My friend Jake Frampton told me something most interesting this evening. According to

Jake, larger city newspapers keep autobiographical files on prominent people in a department called "the morgue." On occasion, reporters are asked to go to the department and write obituaries on individuals not yet dead. These articles are filed away until needed.

Jake and I talked about this. What would be written about us . . . or about friends or family members? A good friend of mine once suggested, "Write what you think you would like your obituary to read—and then try to live up to it."

Wise advice.

Friday October 15

What riches are ours in the world of nature, from the majesty of a distant peak to the fragile beauty of a tiny flower, and all without cost to us, the beholders! No man is poor who has watched a sunrise or keeps a mountain in his heart.

Esther Baldwin York

Saturday October 16

Recent Saturday afternoons for our family have been devoted to university football games. My great-grandson Justin is enjoying much success with his team and the rest of the family is delighting in being a large cheering section for Justin and his teammates. I know how much George would have enjoyed these games. We often used to attend local high school games to watch sons of friends and neighbours play.

George found this interesting bit of trivia many years ago. Did you know that football was once an illegal sport? In 1349, Edward III issued a proclamation that forbade the playing of football because people were neglecting their archery in favour of this more exciting game.

In those days, football was played much differently.

There were no set rules and no referee. The goals could be set many miles apart and players could use any method to get the ball. As a result, broken limbs or fractured skulls were quite common injuries.

Football was also a year-round event. It was "The Game" on the Eve of Lent. In many areas every able-bodied man was ordered to take part in that "game of the year" and it often lasted all day.

I do enjoy the games but I believe that three or four hours at a time is plenty for me.

Sunday October 17

Beyond the circle of the sea,
When voyaging is past,
We seek our final port in Thee;
O bring us home at last.

In Thee we trust, what e'er befall;
Thy sea is great, our boats are small.

Henry Van Dyke

Monday October 18

The secret of a good memory is attention, and attention to a subject depends upon our interest in it. We rarely forget that which has made a deep impression on our minds.

Tryon Edwards

Tuesday October 19

People speak lovingly of the "good old days," but I'm sure that the years have dimmed their memories.

As preparations were made for winter, we had to keep a full wood box and chop and stack enough wood to last through even the coldest of winters. We needed to make enough preserves and jellies, and store vegetables in the cold room. Eiderdown quilts were taken out of mothballs, and screens were replaced by storm windows.

I, for one, am happy to enjoy the "good NOW days."

Wednesday October 20

As one grows older . . . there is time to observe and appreciate. A walk in the fields, a sudden spring shower, a beautiful shimmering snow-

storm in winter, the quiet beauty of a sunset, the sound of a child's voice—all these and many more impressions intertwine themselves gently with one's thoughts . . . . Take time to see all the beauty that you have been missing through the hurrying years.

What wise advise from Preston Bradley.

Thursday October 21

Friends and I attended a most interesting meeting for seniors at our church today. It was a fellowship meeting that we regularly hold but the speaker asked us to reflect on some very thought-provoking questions. Why not see how you would answer these questions?

1. If I could start my life over knowing what I know now, what would I do differently? What would I *not* change?
2. Have I lost touch with anyone? What's keeping me from calling them?
3. If I had an extra hour of free time each day, how would I spend it?
4. Do I worry about things I can't control?
5. Am I having enough fun? Do I laugh every day?
6. Am I making the most of every day?

Friday October 22

October woodlands cry for time to wait;
The beauty-wakened heart cries out to share
This wonderland before it's too late,
Before the frosty limbs stand grey and bare.
Mary E. Linton

Saturday October 23

Sometimes we are guilty of passing negative judgment on others who look, think or talk differently. Often these appraisals are completely incorrect.

George Westinghouse, a genius whom many feel was as brilliant as Thomas Edison, was deemed "dull, backward and impractical" by his teachers, and asked to leave college. Before the age of 20, he had been awarded his first patent for a rotary steam engine. Shortly thereafter he devised a mechanism that could put derailed trains back on the tracks. This device was purchased by almost every railroad in the United States. George Westinghouse also produced an individual empire that would last for generations. He had more than 400 patents and, at the time of his death, was producing a motor-driven wheelchair that would simplify life for those who, like himself, were disabled. Had Westinghouse listened to others, he may have given up and an amazingly productive life would have been wasted.

Sunday October 24

This is the day the Lord hath made; we will rejoice and be glad in it.

Psalm 118:24

Monday October 25

Jack Frost paints a portrait of beauty
With colours so vivid and bright;
It's framed with a purple misty haze
And draped in a frosty night.

There was a touch of frost last night, really giving a feel of the cooler weather to come. As much as I enjoy the beauty of autumn, each passing year makes me less anxious to see winter arrive!

I guess my age is showing!

Tuesday October 26

When we do the best we can, we never know what miracle is wrought in our life, or in the life of another.

Helen Keller

Wednesday October 27

Our concern should be not how long we live, but how we live. God holds the length; we hold the manner of living.

Ann Allan

Thursday October 28

The crowning fortune of a man is to be born to some pursuit which finds him in employment and happiness, whether it be to make baskets, or broadswords, or canals, or statues, or songs.

Ralph Waldo Emerson

Friday October 29

I like these thoughts from Jacob M. Braude:

Whoever you are, there is some young person who thinks you are perfect.
There is some work that will never be done if you don't do it.

There is someone who would miss you if you
were gone.
There is a place you alone can fill.

Saturday October 30

As we make ready for Hallowe'en, my son-in-law Bruce is carving our jack-o-lantern with my great-grandchildren Michael and Bethany. My thanks go to the unknown author for these lines on this special night.

"I wonder," said the big pumpkin
Who was round and quite fat,
While nestling at the cornstalk's feet,

With whom he loved to chat,
"If I should be a pumpkin pie,
Or since I'm built just right,
Should I be a jack-o-lantern
On this Hallowe'en night?

"I can't decide which I should be . . . .
A lantern or a pie."
And so he sat and thought and thought,
But as he gave a sigh
A small boy pounced and homeward ran
And scooped the pumpkin out,
From which his mother made a pie
And then with a glad shout
He carved a happy pumpkin face,
One with a toothy grin,
And he found a stubby candle
To light him from within.
On Hallowe'en night the pumpkin
Graced the table as a pie,
And carved as a jack-o-lantern
He smiled at passersby.

Sunday October 31

Blessed are they that have not seen, and yet have believed.

John 20:29

November

All Saints' Day

Although we were few in number at this morning's special service for All Saints' Day, I enjoyed this hymn very much.

Who are these like stars appearing,
Those, before God's throne who stand?
Each a golden crown is wearing,
Who are all this glorious band?
Alleluia, hark! They sing,
Praising loud the heavenly King.

Who are all these in dazzling brightness,
Clothed in God's own righteousness?
These whose robes of purest whiteness,
Shall their lustre still possess,
Still untouched by time's rude hand;
Whence come all this glorious band?

These are those who have contended
For the Saviour's honour long,
Wrestling on till life was ended,

Following not the sinful throng;
These, who well the fight sustained,
Triumph through the Lamb have gained.
Rev. H. T. Shenk

Tuesday November 2

Some years ago, the award-winning actress Katharine Hepburn gave us these thoughts on growing old:

I think we're finally at a point where we've learned to see death with a sense of humour. I have to. When you're my age, it's as if you're a car. First a tire blows, and then you get that fixed. Then the headlight goes, and you get that fixed. And then one day, you drive into a shop, and the man says, "Sorry Miss, they don't have this make anymore."

I suppose I'm still hoping that I can get parts for some time to come.

Wednesday November 3

Don't spend ten dollars' worth of energy on a ten cent problem. There are millions of want-to's and have-to's in life. Ultimately, these pressures create stress only when your time and energy-spending decisions aren't consistent with your goals, beliefs and values.
Dr. D.A. Tubesing

Thursday November 4

The people who think they must always speak the truth often overlook another good choice—silence.

Friday November 5

Whether or not you are a student of history, you have probably, at some time, marvelled at the changes that have taken place from the earliest age until now. From the time of creation, change has been continuous. People have been forced to adapt themselves to this rapid change in order to survive.

However, never before in the history of mankind have the changes come as rapidly as they have in the last hundred years. There is a greater gap between the way young people live and the way their grandparents lived than there was between Sir John A. Macdonald and Julius Caesar's.

We must continually adapt ourselves to the changed order of things—keeping our sense of values while keeping our minds resilient and open to new viewpoints and attitudes.

For those of us who are elderly, this is sometimes a difficult thing to do. I am the first to admit that I don't always adapt well to change. For me, adapting requires a real and continuous effort.

I am willing to make that effort because I think

it is important for us all to live in the present, and to contribute what we can to the times in which we live.

Saturday November 6

Someone once observed that there are only three types of people: those who make things happen, those who watch things happen and those who say, "What happened?"

Sunday November 7

My voice shalt thou hear in the morning, O Lord; in the morning will I direct my prayer unto thee, and will look up.

Psalm 5:3

Monday November 8

My son-in-law John, a minister, spends much time in sermon preparation. He likes to be concise as he makes his point, assuming that brevity will hold everyone's attention for the full length of his sermon.

He likes to tell this story: A minister, whose sermons were often lengthy, noticed that one member of his congregation often fell asleep during the presentation.

One Sunday, the minister decided to remedy this problem. In a whisper he asked all members of the congregation who wished to go to heaven to rise. Everyone got up except for the sleeping man in row three. Then, the minister said in a very loud voice, "All those who want to be with the devil, please rise."

The sleepy man, startled awake, jumped to his feet, and saw the angry minister standing in the pulpit.

"Well, preacher," the man said, "I'm not sure what we're voting on but apparently you and I are the only ones for it."

Tuesday November 9

Good friends of mine, Marilyn and Larry Spicer, were out at a restaurant for dinner one evening when Larry began to choke on a piece of the roast beef he was eating. At first he simply clutched his throat while attempting to cough—but it was to no avail. As his level of panic rose, he stood up and Marilyn attempted to use the Heimlich manoeuvre. Her first attempt was unsuccessful, but a gentleman at the next table, seeing what was happening, came over to Larry and took Marilyn's place behind Larry. With just one sharp upward thrust of his fist to Larry's abdomen, he used air in Larry's lungs to blow out the obstruction. It was a very frightening experience that had a happy ending.

This simple technique has already saved thousands of lives. Dr. Henry J. Heimlich developed his method in the 1970s and it may be done in several different ways, depending on the type of choking case. For example, if you are alone and choking, use your own fist and other hand for the inward–upward jab, or press your abdomen quickly and forcefully into a rounded corner of a table or the back of a chair. Almost any blunt object that provides pressure under the breast-bone will cause the lungs to expel an obstruction.

Fortunately, restaurants in North America display an illustrated poster demonstrating the Heimlich manoeuvre, so incidents of choking to death have become rare.

If you haven't learned how to do this life-saving manoeuvre now is the time!

Wednesday November 10

The richest man in the world is not the one who still has the first dollar he ever earned. It's the man who still has his first friend.

Marsha Mason

Thursday November 11

Remembrance Day

Marg and I were at our local elementary school today, and we were very pleased to be a part of the Remembrance Day program. One of the loveliest portions of the presentation came when the entire school joined together to sing "Let There Be Peace on Earth." It brought tears to my eyes.

Let there be peace on Earth,
And let it begin with me.
Let there be peace on Earth
The peace that was meant to be.

With God as our Father,
Brothers all are we,
Let me walk with my brother,
In perfect harmony.

Let peace begin with me,
Let this be the moment now.
With every step I take,
Let this be my solemn vow.

To take each moment and live each moment
In peace, eternally.
Let there be peace on Earth,
And let it begin with me.

Jill Jackson
and Sy Miller

Friday November 12

One of the indisputable facts of life is that every man must have a system of values if he hopes to live life to its best. All good things do not have the same value. All facts and reasons are not of equal importance. All joys are not equally satisfying. All happiness does not have the same survival value. The man who has truly solved the problem of life is one who recognizes these differences.

Saturday November 13

I thank the unknown author for these lines for today.

Give me the simple things close to my home,
The things that are familiar, old and dear,
I do not have to wander far, or roam
The Seven Seas—when I have splendour
here.

Give me a crackling flame upon the grate,
And the warm smell of bread upon the fire.
I do not have to ride abroad in state
To find the very core of heart's desire.

A shining teapot—friendly hands to pour
And jam that smells of grape from our own
vine.
Could any noble king desire more?
I am a king myself, for these are mine.

Let those who will seek promised lands afar,
For treasures so remote I shed no tears.
Why should I strive to reach a distant star
When heaven with all its beauty is right here!

Sunday November 14

Be strong and of good courage; be not afraid, neither be thou dismayed: for the Lord thy God is with thee whithersoever thou goest.

Joshua 1:9

Monday November 15

With age we become responsible for what's in our heads—the character of the memories there, the music we are familiar with, the storehouse of the books we have read, the people we can call, the scenery we know and love. Our memories become our dreams.

Edgar Hoagland

Tuesday November 16

One of Marshall's and Jamie's neighbours is a real estate agent. I hope that she has a good sense of humour as Marshall gave her this list of "Real Estate Advertising Interpretations."

"Much Potential"—Steer clear unless you have an unlimited supply of money.

"Unique City Home"—Used to be a warehouse.

"Daring Design"—Still a warehouse.

"Sophisticated"—Black walls and no windows.

"Must See to Believe"—A completely accurate statement!

Wednesday November 17

Mark Twain made this wise observation:

Life would be infinitely happier if we could only be born at the age of eighty and gradually approach eighteen.

Thursday November 18

One of the best-loved hymns, "Blest Be the Ties That Bind," written by the Reverend John Fawcett, has an interesting story to its composition.

Reverend Fawcett was the minister of a small Baptist church in the village of Wainsgate, in Yorkshire, England. He had come to the church as a newly ordained young man of 26 and had served his congregation for seven years. The £200 a year salary had made it a struggle to raise his large family. And so, as much as his congregation had loved him and he had loved them in return, when he received a call to a much larger church in London (at a greater salary) he accepted.

Some days later when he and his family had packed all their belongings into wagons for the 200-mile journey to London, the Fawcetts had second thoughts. They really did not want to leave. At the last minute John climbed out of the wagon and said, "We aren't leaving!"

For the next 60 years Reverend Fawcett

remained at the small Wainsgate Church. When he passed away in 1816, he left very little in the way of material things to his children, but he gave to them and to the world one of the most beloved hymns, "Bless Be the Ties That Bind."

Friday November 19

Happiness exists where there is, in addition to the things that bring satisfaction and contentment, a conscious awareness that one has these things. Most of us have the first qualification of happiness—we have an abundance of blessings. It is in the second area that we fall short: we fail to recognize the fact that we have these things. Through such recognition we achieve happiness.

Saturday November 20

Marg, Bruce and I went for a drive today and our route took us to an area just north of Paris, Ontario. While there, Bruce took us to see the Paris Plains Church, a most unusual cobblestone-walled building that used the common fieldstones abundant in the farmers' fields in Paris and the Brantford area.

In the 1850s, Levi Boughton came from Rochester, New York, to Paris, Ontario, bringing with him a unique construction technique that dated back to the ancient Roman occupation in England.

The stones, usually dolomite or limestone, were passed through a ring to ensure uniformity of size and shape. They were then laid in level courses to construct walls of incredibly straight cobblestones—quite extraordinary to behold. The contractor for the church was Philo Hull, who also constructed many other buildings in Paris, using the same technique. However, as brick-making made construction so much less expensive, Boughton's cobblestone style died out. The church is a rare beauty that one needs to see to appreciate.

Sunday November 21

A new commandment I give unto you. That ye love one another; as I have loved you, that ye also love one another.

By this shall all men know that ye are my disciples, if ye have love one to another.

John 13:34–35

Monday November 22

Marshall and Jamie attended an anniversary party for good friends this evening. I enjoyed this story that Marshall told at the celebration:

I congratulate you on your 15th anniversary and I would like to tell you of another couple who recently celebrated their 75th anniversary. The gentleman was 100 years old, and when asked how he managed to look so well at his age, he answered, 'My wife and I have been married for 75 years now. On our wedding night, we promised one another that whenever we had a fight, the one who proven wrong would go out and take a walk. I have been in the outdoors in all weather—continuously—for 75 years.'

Tuesday November 23

Harvest days are over,
Nights are growing cold,
There's a threat of winter
As the year grows old.

I thought of these lines this morning as I looked out at our first heavy frost of the season. November has always felt so dreary to me—all browns and greys; autumn colours gone but no white snow yet to brighten the ground.

Far to the northward, gleaming
Northern lights appear;
Everything is telling
That wintertime is near.

Wednesday November 24

The miracles of nature do not seem miracles because they are so common. If no one had ever seen a flower, even a dandelion would be the most startling event in the world.

Thursday November 25

Today is the day that our American friends celebrate their Thanksgiving.

Thanksgiving is a time for remembering
And each time this day draws near—
The hearts of mankind join in grateful praise
At this special time of year.

V.K. Oliver

Friday November 26

None of us knows what is ahead. The important thing is to use today wisely and well, and face tomorrow eagerly and cheerfully, and with certainty that we shall be equal to what it brings.

Saturday November 27

A friend of mine, Adrien Koert, had an amusing experience this week. Adrien and his wife made a trip north for a short visit to their cottage. When they arrived they found that the water pump wasn't working and they had no running water. Adrien called a local plumber and was pleased when he arrived in less than an hour. Following him to the pump house, Adrien watched as the plumber used his blowtorch to heat the pipe and in short order the water was running again. The bill for the visit was $20, which Adrien paid cheerfully.

The next morning, the water was stopped again but instead of calling the plumber, Adrien decided he could just as easily use his own torch to get the water flowing.

He started the torch and turned it on to the pipe in what he thought was the same way that the plumber had done. In short order the water was flowing—and spraying all over the pump house!

Adrien put in an emergency call to the plumber, who surveyed the scene and said wryly, "Well, you can call me and pay only $20 to have your plumbing fixed . . . or you can fix it yourself and *then* call me to repair your work and that will cost you $90.00"

Sunday November 28

First Sunday in Advent

The fourth Sunday before Christmas marks the beginning of Advent and, for many families, this is the start of the Christmas season. This hymn from Frances Ridley Havergal was always one of my favourites for the season.

Thou art coming, O my Saviour,
Thou art coming, O my King,
In Thy beauty all-resplendent,
In thy glory all-transcendent;
Well may we rejoice and sing;

Coming:—in the opening east
Herald brightness slowly swells;
Coming:—O my glorious Priest
Hear we not thy golden Bells?

Monday November 29

Enjoy the little things, for one day you may look back and realize they were the big things.

Robert Brault

Tuesday November 30

Kindness is the language which the deaf can hear and the blind can see.

Mark Twain

December

Last night we had our first snowfall and I was reminded of this poem from Archibald Lampman.

Snow

White are the far off-plains, and white
The fading forests grow;
The wind dies out along the height,
And denser still the snow,
A gathering weight on roof and tree,
Falls down scarcely audibly.

The road before me smoothes and fills
Apace, and all about
The fences dwindle, and the hills
Are blotted slowly out;
The naked trees loom spectrally
Into the dim white sky.

The meadows are far-sheeted streams
Lie still without a sound;
Like some soft minister of dreams
The snow-fall hoods me round;

In wood and water, earth and air,
A silence everywhere.

Save when at lonely intervals
Some farmer's sleigh urged on,
With rustling runners and sharp bells,
Swings by me and is gone;
Or from the empty waste I hear
A sound remote and clear;

The barking of a dog, or call
To cattle, sharply pealed,
Borne echoing from some wayside stall
Or barnyard far afield;
The all is silent, and the snow
Falls settling soft and slow.

The evening deepens, and the grey
Folds closer earth and sky;
The world seems shrouded far away;
Its noises sleep, and I,
As secret as yon buried stream,
Plod dumbly on, and dream.

Thursday December 2

Our creator would never have made such lovely days and have given us the deep hearts to enjoy them, above and beyond all thought, unless we were meant to be immortal.

Friday December 3

Each year at this time, we all have to give much thought to our Christmas shopping.

For those of us on a fixed budget this can be rather challenging. Each year it seems to take me longer and longer to find inexpensive but thoughtful gifts for my family and friends. This year I have an idea that I hope will please everyone. I have spent many hours going through boxes of photographs and have chosen a half-dozen or more for each person. They are mostly from family outings or special occasions, such as birthdays or anniversaries. I am going to our local dollar store to find an album for each person and then I will arrange the photos in the albums with a brief note attached to each picture. I hope the pictures and notes will bring back some happy memories of times that we've spent together. The rest of the album will be theirs to fill as they wish.

Saturday December 4

Our family got together today for an afternoon of baking cookies. With so many of our family coming together to celebrate Christmas, Marg decided that it would be fun to do some baking together and, in that way, we could be sure that we were not all making the same kind of cookies or cakes.

The other nice thing about baking together was

that we could make dozens of extra cookies that we could use for our annual "cookie exchange" parties that we attend each year.

Even chores become pleasant tasks at this time of year.

Sunday December 5

Second Sunday in Advent

Behold, a virgin shall be with child, and shall bring forth a son, and they shall call his name Emmanuel, which being interpreted is, God with us.

Matthew 1:23

Monday December 6

The world being as it is, many families have loved ones widely scattered and unable to get together during the holiday season. How well I remember a letter I received from dear friends some years ago, who solved the problem of loneliness at Christmas. I'd like to share their thoughts with you:

As you know, Edna, our family is scattered across the country and, at this time of year, we find ourselves missing them all very much. This year we decided that, instead of sitting around feeling sorry for ourselves, we would find things to do that would keep us busy and yet be helpful to others.

We have been having a wonderful time. One day we helped supervise a school class trip to a Christmas presentation. On another day, we took several handicapped youngsters to see the Christmas lights downtown. This week we are taking residents from our local nursing home to do some Christmas shopping, and, later in the month, we are going to sing carols with our choir at the children's hospital.

It has been a wonderful tonic for us. Although we still miss our children and their families, we are enjoying the fellowship and love that comes with giving of ourselves.

What a wonderful idea for us all!

Tuesday December 7
I enjoy Henry Van Dyke's analysis of gift-giving:

If every gift is the token of a personal thought, a friendly feeling, an unselfish interest, the feeling, the interest, may remain long after the gift is forgotten.

Wednesday December 8
Stars over snow,
And in the west, a planet

Swinging below a star—
Look for that lovely thing and you'll find it,
It is not far—
It never will be far.

Sara Teasdale

Thursday December 9

All across Canada at this time of year, numerous light festivals celebrate the holiday season. One of the loveliest of these festivals is in Ladysmith, British Columbia, a small town just south of Nanaimo on Vancouver Island.

Originally known as Oyster Harbour, the town was established by James Dunsmuir in 1899. When the British won a major victory in the Boer War in South Africa, Dunsmuir renamed his town after Ladysmith in Natal Province.

The Ladysmith Festival of Lights is the most spectacular on Vancouver Island. It always opens on the last Thursday in November with hundreds of thousands of decorative lights, a parade, spectacular fireworks and a spaghetti dinner fundraiser that attracts more than 450 people.

The festival runs right through the month of December, and visitors come from all over the island and the mainland to see this breathtaking display.

For those of us living in other parts of Canada, there are many other displays to see, and it is

WINTER FUN

possible to find out about them either by calling your local chamber of commerce or by searching on-line under Canadian Light Festivals.

Friday December 10

Here's some good advice for this time of year:

If your cup runneth over, let someone else runneth the car.

Saturday December 11

We spent many hours today at our church bazaar. I marvel at the ingenuity of our friends and neighbours; many of the articles at this sale are handmade by the parishioners.

Each year we hold a raffle and this event is very near and dear to my heart. Back in 1996, my friend Betty, who was an invalid for many years, made a magnificent pinecone Christmas tree. The tree stands about two feet tall and is decorated with miniature white lights, tiny red bows and garlands of small white beads, all hand-strung by Betty.

After she had completed her work, she boxed the tree with a card that read, "Please make sure Edna McCann has this tree for the Christmas raffle."

Betty passed away before the Christmas bazaar was held, but her creation was raffled off for more than $1,500, a most fitting tribute to a kind, gentle lady.

As if that wasn't wonderful enough, the winner of the tree returned the creation the next year to be used as a fund-raiser again. The tradition has continued and this year, we will raffle this beautiful decoration for the eighth straight year.

Even after her death this selfless soul still goes on giving.

Sunday December 12

Third Sunday in Advent

The Advent of our King
Our prayers must now employ,
And we must hymns of welcome sing
In strains of holy joy.

All glory to the Son
Who comes to see us free
With Father, Spirit ever One
Through all eternity.

Rev. John Chandler

Monday December 13

One of the loveliest observances at this time of year is St. Lucia Day or, as the Swedes call it, Luciadagen. This festival of light, which marks the beginning of the Christmas season for the people of the Scandinavian countries of Denmark, Norway and Sweden, is held on December 13, although the original St. Lucia Day used to fall on the solstice.

Legend has it that St. Lucia was betrothed against her will to a pagan nobleman. He claimed that her beautiful eyes haunted him day and night. In an attempt to end the engagement, she supposedly cut out her eyes and sent them to her suitor. God rewarded her sacrifice by giving her even more beautiful eyes. For this she is known as the patron saint of the blind.

"Lucia" means light and all the traditional ceremonies for the day centre on a beautiful St. Lucia, dressed in a shining white robe and lighting the darkness with a crown of candles.

This tradition is carried on in many areas of our country where there are large numbers of Scandinavian Canadians.

Many families enjoy a smorgasbord dinner, known as Julbord feast, and a Lucia procession is led by the "Lucia Bride," a young girl who wears a white robe, a crimson sash and a metal crown covered with white candles. The other children in the procession carry single candles, and it is a beautiful sight in the early evening darkness.

Tuesday December 14

Our local high school students came carolling this evening to collect canned goods for the

Christmas basket drive. Their singing was wonderful, and I couldn't help but think that the future is in good hands.

Wednesday December 15

This is the time of year when unexpected company is a regular happening. It's always good to have a number of easily fixed snacks on hand to serve at moments notice. Young and old alike enjoy this one:

Pizza Dip

1 (8 oz./250 g) package of cream cheese
1 small tin of pizza sauce
1 (4.2 oz./125 g) can chopped ripe olives
1 pkg. pepperoni, diced
1 small can sliced mushrooms, drained, or
   3/4 cup (175 mL) fresh mushrooms
1 cup (250 mL) Mozzarella cheese, shredded

1. Preheat the oven to 350°F (180°C). Soften the cream cheese and spread it on a 9 x 13 inch (12 x 33 cm) Pyrex dish. (You may soften the cheese further by adding 1 tbsp. [15 mL] of milk)
2. Generously spread the pizza sauce over the layer of cheese. Top with olives, pepperoni and mushrooms.
3. Sprinkle the shredded Mozzarella over all.

4. Put in oven until heated through and the cheese topping is bubbling. Serve with taco chips, bagel chips or sliced Italian bread.

You can also add chopped or sliced red peppers, or green onions.

Thursday December 16

Children enjoy being a part of the preparations for the season. For those of you with children, grandchildren or great-grandchildren, I offer a few ideas that youngsters seem to enjoy.

In our family we like to go to a local farm to choose our Christmas tree. Even the youngest children enjoy picking the "perfect pine."

Of course, decorating the tree is something that appeals to children as well. In our family, each child is given the chance to select one new decoration each year that is just for them. The decoration selected has their name and the year written on it, and they enjoy placing all their own ornaments on the tree. For the rest of us adults, it's fun to see how the children's taste in ornaments changes over the years.

Many decorations may be homemade. A trip to the library to find Christmas craft books will give you any number of age-appropriate crafts to make with youngsters.

Children of all ages can help with Christmas baking; the older children measure ingredients while the younger ones stir. A few inexpensive cookie cutters add that special festive touch that children love.

A trip to see the light displays in your area is an activity that will be enjoyed by all ages.

Whatever you and your loved ones choose to do at this special time of year will make lasting memories for all.

Friday December 17

On this 101st anniversary of the Wright brothers' flight at Kitty Hawk, I offer these lines in tribute to their accomplishment. This is the telegram sent to their father, the Reverend Milton Wright, on December 17, 1903.

Success / four flights Thursday morning / all against twenty-one-mile wind / started from level with engine power alone / longest fifty nine seconds / inform press / home Christmas.

Saturday December 18

Are you willing to believe that love is the strongest thing in the world—stronger than hate, stronger than evil, stronger than death—and that the blessed life which began in Bethlehem nineteen hundred years ago, is the image and brightness of the Eternal Love? Then you can keep Christmas.

And if you can keep it for a day, why not always?

But you can never keep it alone.

Henry Van Dyke

Sunday December 19

Fourth Sunday in Advent

Hark the glad sound! The Saviour comes,
The Saviour promised long:
Let every heart prepare a throne,
And every voice a song.

Rev. P. Doddridge

Monday December 20

I find it interesting to note how the Christmas season is celebrated in different areas of our country and in other countries around the world. And yet the underlying thought of each celebration is the same. It is the season when "it is more blessed to give than to receive." It is the time of year when the greatest pleasure you get is the joy you give.

Tuesday December 21

Today we welcome a new season—winter.

Winter has come and the trees are now bare,
You feel all her wrath on the cold frosty air,

The bird songs are silent . . . the flow'rs are
   gone,
There's nothing to hear but the wind's plain-
   tive song.

When north winds are blowing and snow fills
   the air,
There's nothing more cozy or lovely to share
Than a big roaring fire . . . some well chosen
   friends,
And the warm hearty welcome a fireside
   extends.

Wednesday December 22

The grand essentials of life are something to do,
something to love and something to hope for.

Thursday December 23

Hanukkah, the Jewish celebration in this
month of the year, is a special time for children. While the candles burn in the menorah, it
is a time for songs and games.

One of the most popular of the games is played
with a four-sided top, known as a dreidel. On
each of the four sides of the dreidel there is one
Hebrew letter—Nu, Shin, Gimmel and Heh—
representing the words "new gadol hayeh sham"
or "a great miracle happened here."

Children often play the dreidel game with
Hanukkah "gelt," coins made of chocolate and

wrapped in gold foil. Each child places a set number of coins in a common pot. Then they, in turn, spin the dreidel and when the top stops, the letter that is upright determines the outcome. Nu means nothing is added to the pot; Shin means one coin must be added to the pot; Gimmel means the player may take all of the coins in the pot; and Heh means the player may take half the coins in the pot (if a player lands on Gimmel and takes all the coins, each of the players must ante in two coins for the game to continue). The game ends when each player has spun a predetermined number of spins or a time limit has been reached.

May I wish all of my Jewish friends a Happy Hanukkah and all the joys of this special time of year.

Friday December 24

> Hark! The herald angels sing,
> Glory to the new-born King . . .

Saturday December 25

Christmas Day

Christmas is a time of traditions and each family has its own set of customs that have passed from generation to generation. Of course your traditions depend upon your roots, each country around the world having different ideas for this joyous celebration.

A tradition that our family has developed over the past few years is our Christmas Day trip to our local nursing home. Often the home is short-staffed and those staff members who are working can use extra hands to do any number of small tasks that will make the day happier for the residents. Even the children participate as they sing carols or push wheelchairs from room to room.

This has become a very special part of our Christmas Day, something that I hope will continue for many, many years.

Sunday December 26

> Angels from the realms of glory,
> Wing your flight o'er all the earth;
> Ye who sang creations story,
> Now proclaim Messiah's birth:
> Come and worship,
> Worship Christ, the new-born King.

Monday December 27

Be not anxious about tomorrow. Do today's duty, fight today's temptations and do not weaken and distract yourself by looking forward to things which you cannot see, and could not understand if you saw them.

Charles Kingsley

Tuesday December 28

The man who is too old to learn was probably always too old to learn.

H.S. Haskins

Wednesday December 29

Intelligence, reflection and judgment reside in old men. . . . Age, especially an honoured old age, has so great authority that this is of more value than all the pleasures of youth. . . .

Old age is the consummation of life, just as of a play. . . . The harvest of old age is the recollection and abundance of blessings previously secured.

Marcus Tullius Cicero

Thursday December 30

Good-bye, Old Year! Tried, trusty friend, thy tale at last is told; O New Year! Write thou thine for us in lines of brightest gold.

Friday December 31

I know an elderly lady who says that she has made it a habit to expect every morning, when she awakens, to have a glorious day.

As this year ends and we look to the year ahead why shouldn't we, as my friend does, expect each day of the coming year to be a wonderful one? More often than not a great expectation will bring the very things we are awaiting.

A Happy New Year to you all!